PRAISE FOR *SPIRI*

"Welch opens up a new way to think about the realm of spirits and ghosts. By normalizing how we interact with the energy of those who have crossed the barrier between living and dead, Welch makes the supernatural natural. This is a book all psychic mediums need."

—Arwen Lynch Poe, US Games writer and author

"Welch takes you on a deep dive into the brightest and darkest of spirits that move among us … *Spirits Unveiled* is an essential read for anyone interested in taking a fresh look at spirits."

—Jeff Pulver, entrepreneur and founder of over 450 startups, including Pulver.com, pulveREDU, Vonage, VON Coalition, and Zula

"By sharing her stories, offering answers to many common questions, and clearing up misconceptions, Michelle Welch shares new ways of understanding spirits, angels, and ghosts. In this informative book she shines a guiding light on how to connect to and communicate with these powerful realms of energy."

—Amy Zerner and Monte Farber, authors of *The Psychic Circle* and *The Enchanted Spellboard*

"*Spirits Unveiled* gives readers clear definitions, personal stories, and exercises to engage with beings living in the other realms. Michelle is a professional and her advice can help anyone connect to the realm of the spirit!"

—Jaymi Elford, author of *Tarot Inspired Life*

"Welch lifts the lacy curtain and reveals everything you need to know about ghosts, angels, departed loved ones, Ascended Masters, and other-worldly guides. Her unique exercises will help you easily connect to the other side … A must-have book for anyone interested in working with spirits."

—Theresa Reed, author of *Tarot: No Questions Asked*

"*Spirits Unveiled* provides an up-to-date and easy-to-read blueprint for beginners and the well versed in the Spirit world alike."

—Fatima Mbodj, author of *New Orleans Oracle Deck*

"A spiritually daring book…Welch draws you in and keeps you transfixed and spiritually renewed."

—Dr. Toni Muñoz-Hunt, doctor of philosophy and literature at the University of Texas at Dallas

"Fascinating, practical, and empowering…A must have for magical souls and mystery seekers."

—Sasha Graham, author of *The Magic of Tarot* and *Dark Wood Tarot*

"A fascinating read…There is so much information yet felt effortless to get through."

—Sasha Marchetti, Afterlife Astrology

"If you've never had a spirit encounter before and would like to contact the parallel universes around you, or you have met spirits and just want to deepen your understanding of them, *Spirits Unveiled* is the guidebook you have been looking for."

—Madame Pamita, author of *Baba Yaga's Book of Witchcraft*

"Michelle offers techniques that replace superstition and fear with truth and empowerment in how we work with spirits. Michelle's work represents an important step forward in the way we think about the relationship between the physical and spiritual."

—James Divine, founder of The Divine Hand Palmistry

"A remarkable new book that shows us how we can live and interact with the spirit world NOW, while we are embodied…Michelle helps the everyday person step forward and learn how they too can have these life-altering, mystical, magical experiences."

—Dr. Amy Robbins, doctor of clinical psychology and host of *Life, Death, and the Space Between* podcast

"Your questions on the greater Mysteries are revealed in this incredible, insightful guide to angels, ghosts, and everything earthly and celestial on the spectrum of energy. Beautiful, inspiring, and full of love, *Spirits Unveiled* is a treasure of a read."

—Benebell Wen, author of *Holistic Tarot*, *The Tao of Craft*, and *Spirit Keeper Tarot*

Spirits Unveiled

ABOUT THE AUTHOR

Michelle Welch is the owner of the SoulTopia, LLC chain of metaphysical stores, where she offers a variety of services as a psychic medium. She is a licensed attorney and has lent her intuitive abilities to notable court cases. Michelle is the host of the *SoulWhat* podcast and the Michelle SoulTopia YouTube channel. As the owner of the Northwest Tarot Symposium and The International Divination Event, she has also presented at many other events, including the Reader's Studio and the International New Age Trade Show. As seen on *CBS News*, *Inside Edition*, *The Jenny McCarthy Show*, *Coast to Coast*, *The Morning After*, *Good Morning Texas*, and much more. Michelle is the author of *The Magic of Connection* published by Llewelyn Worldwide. Visit her at MichelleWelch.com and MySoulTopia.com.

Spirits Unveiled

A Fresh Perspective on Angels, Guides, Ghosts & More

Michelle Welch

WITH A FOREWORD BY ETHONY DAWN

Llewellyn Publications
Woodbury, Minnesota

First Edition
First Printing, 2022

Book design by Colleen McLaren
Cover design by Shannon McKuhen

Llewellyn Publications is a registered trademark of Llewellyn
    Worldwide Ltd.

Library of Congress Cataloging-in-Publication Data
Names: Welch, Michelle (Spiritualist), author.
Title: Spirits unveiled : a fresh perspective on angels, guides, ghosts &
    more / Michelle Welch.
Description: Woodbury, Minnesota : Llewellyn Worldwide, Ltd, 2022. |
    Includes bibliographical references and index.
Identifiers: LCCN 2022009105 (print) | LCCN 2022009106 (ebook) | ISBN
    9780738771380 | ISBN 9780738771557 (ebook)
Subjects: LCSH: Spirits.
Classification: LCC BF1552 .W45 2022 (print) | LCC BF1552 (ebook) | DDC
    133.9—dc23/eng/20220325
LC record available at https://lccn.loc.gov/2022009105
LC ebook record available at https://lccn.loc.gov/2022009106

Llewellyn Worldwide Ltd. does not participate in, endorse, or have any authority or responsibility concerning private business transactions between our authors and the public.

All mail addressed to the author is forwarded but the publisher cannot, unless specifically instructed by the author, give out an address or phone number.

Any internet references contained in this work are current at publication time, but the publisher cannot guarantee that a specific location will continue to be maintained. Please refer to the publisher's website for links to authors' websites and other sources.

Llewellyn Publications
A Division of Llewellyn Worldwide Ltd.
2143 Wooddale Drive
Woodbury, MN 55125-2989
www.llewellyn.com

Printed in the United States of America

OTHER BOOKS BY MICHELLE WELCH

Pendulum Palooza

*The Magic of Connection: Stop Cutting Cords & Learn to Transform
Negative Energy to Live an Empowered Life*

FORTHCOMING BOOKS BY MICHELLE WELCH

The Magic of Crystals Oracle Deck & Guidebook

Psychic Playbook

To *Wonderful Walker*
GoGo loves you

Contents

Practices

Chapter 9

Chapter 10

Chapter 11

Disclaimer

Anyone reading this book or listening to it in any form hereby acknowledges and is tacitly assumed to have read this disclaimer. This publication contains the opinions and ideas of the author. The information provided herein cannot be given to any degree of certainty or guarantee, and you should not rely on it to make any decision that would affect your legal, financial, or medical condition. If any condition, inquiry, or situation involves the law, finance, or medicine, then you should seek the advice of a licensed or qualified legal, financial, or medical professional. These methods can only facilitate how you cope spiritually with a given situation.

Furthermore, certain jurisdictions require that those in the field of fortune-telling must state *for entertainment purposes only*. To the extent you live in such a jurisdiction, consider yourself on notice thereof. The author and publisher and all of their affiliates specifically disclaim all responsibility for any liability, loss, or risk, personal or otherwise, that is incurred as a consequence, directly or indirectly, of the use and application of any of the contents of this book. The author has endeavored to recreate events, locales, and conversations from her memories and conversations with those involved. Therefore, it reflects her present recollections of experiences over time. In order to maintain anonymity, some names and characteristics have been changed, some events have been compressed, and some dialogue has been recreated.

Gratitude

There are countless people whom I wish to express my gratitude to—this book was a tough one in the living and the writing. Please allow me to limit my thanks to those who specifically helped me with the writing and living of this book. Thank you to ...

Roger Welch—My very own ET. Thanks for ditching your other-worldlies to hang out on Earth with me.

Tyler Scheef, James LaVerse, Trevor Scheef, Val Scheef, Tanner Scheef, Jordan Chandler, William Welch, and Lizzie Welch—You all are such independent spirits. People love to pick on younger generations and that is a mistake with you guys. The multiverse is in good hands with you all. Someday, I might be cool enough to make it into your special group chat.

Llewelyn Worldwide—Thanks to all of you for your expertise and words of wisdom. Angela Wix, Barbara Moore, Michelle Palazallo, Patti Frazee, Alisha Bjorklund, Shannon McKuhen, Colleen McLaren, Sami Sherratt, Kat Neff, and Anna Levine.

Ethony Dawn—Your friendship means so much to me and Roger. Thank you for writing the foreword to my book.

Ashlie Daniel—We have a rare connection shared by those who know what living a life of seeing is truly like. I am glad we are both still here to support one another and that your brother brought us together.

Carla Nichols—You are a lifesaver. You discern truth very clearly, and that is rare.

Dawn Crosby Moore—Your attention to detail and being there to help will never be forgotten.

Mary Gates and Nikki Pere (the sparkle and sunflowers)—Thank you for the texts making sure I was alive.

Leah Curtis—Thank you for reminding me to drink water.

Benebell Wen, Jim Barker, Madame Pamita, and Tracey Natarajan—Thank you for always listening and lending support.

The Colombe Family for always being there. Your gift of the Owinja (star quilt) meant more to me than you will ever know. Star quilts are the most valued gifts of the Sioux people, meant to bestow recognition and honor. I love your Lakota family!

Ashlie Daniel, Tanya Garrett, Sarah Boone, Carlton Griffin, Roger Welch, Lorie Cornelius, Collins Cornelius, Ava Cornelius, Mary Gates, Nicole Pere, Karla Flynn, and Carla Nichols—Thank you for sharing your stories on such personal matters.

Monte Farber and Amy Zerner—Sometimes you meet people, and you wonder how you lived without knowing them. I am so glad you are in my life. You set such a beautiful example for so many to follow of love, hard work, and excellence.

Lory LeBlanc—Thank you for supporting me through some of the darker times as a psychic medium. Spirituality is not always an easy road, and it is great to have those along the way who help you see a path forward.

Judy Hagen—You are the reason I still play amongst the living. You stood by me when very few did. When I was in the depths of despair in a mental hospital, you didn't care what the rumors were; you just loved me unconditionally. You love everyone that way, and anyone lucky enough to have you in their life is a fool to lose you.

The Doctor Who Saved My Life—Thank you so much for convincing me to live. After batteries of tests, you *saw* me, told me I was not of this world, and prevented me from receiving shock therapy. I have had a lot of rough experiences throughout my time as a psychic but thankfully you saw the truth of my pain.

All of you who read my first book and have never stopped supporting me. I know, I remember, and it makes all the difference.

All the SoulTopians who have stood by us. Going all in on a dream is often scarier than any spirits I have ever encountered. Thank you for those who have supported this journey.

Foreword

I met Michelle at Readers Studio in New York in 2018. I was doing what you do at a conference between sessions—shopping—when I found Soultopia's table. As I was perusing all their magical, metaphysical goodies, Michelle introduced herself and we had an instant connection. We spent the rest of the conference talking, laughing, and honestly, making some mischief.

I was immediately impressed with her vibrant spirit and deep wisdom. It was clear to me that she had a lot to share with the world. In 2020, I invited her to facilitate a session at my online conference, Tarot Summer School, and her session was one of the students' favorites.

I was thrilled to see the success of her first book, *The Magic of Connection: Stop Cutting Cords & Learn to Transform Negative Energy to Live an Empowered Life,* and am honored to be asked to write the foreword for this second one. Michelle never ceases to amaze me. Somehow, she manages to write books, create decks, and have three Soultopia locations in Texas. She is a powerhouse.

Spirits Unveiled often mirrors my own experience with spirits. I've spent most of my life working with spirit guides, elementals, ancestors, disincarnates, and other energy frequencies. For me, my journey began when I was very young since I was always extremely sensitive to people, spaces, and any spirits in the world around me.

I found in this book that Michelle is able to define and explore these beings in a way that helps anyone who has just started their connection with them or who has an unexpected "bump" in the night. It's also helpful for more experienced practitioners who work with these entities. Her extensive exercises allow you to actually put into practice the knowledge written in this book. It's not just a book, it's a working guide to the world of spirits.

Growing up, I didn't have an amazing book like this to help me understand what was happening to me. There is a lot of value to be able to put words to concepts that are difficult to grasp. It helps to navigate through the confusing and sometimes scary experiences we have and it also is comforting to know that we are not alone in dealing with these beings.

I hope you and the spirits you choose to work with gain as much out of this incredible book as I did as there is truly something for everyone in this book.

Ethony Dawn
Tarot reader and author of *Your Tarot Court (Read Any Deck with Confidence);* creator of the *Bad Bitches Tarot*

Introduction

For as long as I can remember, I have asked myself why I have such a strong connection with spirits. Why have they revealed themselves to me since I was a child, and why do they continue to show up now? There might not be many things I know with certainty, but one thing I know without a shadow of a doubt—spirits or energetic beings are everywhere. They are all around us, in all shapes, forms, sizes, and kinds—or as they are called in this book, frequencies. If you can see and feel the spirits all around, you will be nodding your head, thinking, *Yes. Finally, someone is writing what I have known all along.*

I am eager to share with you what I, and perhaps many of you, have experienced. I have had many years of seeing, sensing, identifying, interacting, communicating, and connecting with spirits. Sometimes the intense interactions with spirits have nearly destroyed my life, and other times they have saved it. Over time, I have learned to collaborate with all types of spirits by tuning into their unique frequencies. I hope to pass along what I have learned in my lifetime of dealing with nearly every kind of spirit on the frequency spectrum.

This book is not intended as a claim that I have all the answers or am all-knowing. In fact, you will be privy to some moments where I thought my experiences might get the best of me. This book was often painful in the retelling, but I hope it will make you feel as if you have a friend right beside you even when you are in the depths of despair.

Just a couple of weeks ago, during one of my many trips to the emergency room for kidney stones, I watched as a family circled up to pray with the hospital chaplain in the waiting room. I observed a man in blue jeans and a t-shirt walk up and stand between the chaplain and a woman I knew to be the recent widow. It was so moving to watch the woman calm down as the man put his hand on her shoulder. It was equally fascinating to notice the complete unawareness of the chaplain to the presence of the man standing right beside him. The man looked right at me, and we both smiled. I sent him an energetic hug, and the nurse finally called my name. I had waited seven hours to be seen (with three kidney stones). When I got to my room, I knew I had the room of the man who was now in spirit.

Although many types of energy beings (spirits) will be covered in this book, it is written from my vast experiences with the spirits all around us. Thus, it is not meant to serve as an encyclopedia or historical reference to the subject matters discussed. Rather, it is intended to impress upon you how entangled all energy actually is and how to deal with that energy.

THE SPIRITS UNVEILED: A FRESH PERSPECTIVE

The next time you attend a Christmas festival or orchestra event and a beautiful rendition of "Hark! The Herald Angels Sing" is played, do something if you dare. Try pointing at the ceiling and telling everyone the angels are here watching over us. Well, I did that very thing. How do you think that went over? While everyone was quite concerned with what was wrong with me, I would think, *what is wrong with them?* Spirits have been referred to as long as there has been recorded history. However, if you claim to see or sense spirits, that's when things get a little awkward.

As a young child, when I would sing about angels in church or hear about different kinds of spirit beings that I saw distinctly as the person sitting next to me, it was confusing to me that not everyone really expected the angels to be there. As I grew older, I simply assumed people were hypocrites for saying they believed in spirits because they didn't seem to connect with them in any meaningful way. Of course, this was an unfair and harsh judgment. At some point, I realized that some people may not see these spirits or attempt to connect with them because they believe a veil divides the earthly and spiritual realms. I know now that people who are unaware of the spirits all around them are generally not hypocrites; they simply have not learned to adjust their frequency to see or sense these ever-present beings.

Have you heard that the veil is thinner around certain times of the year? Or at a full moon? Consider this: Perhaps the veil is a human construct born out of some form of fear. It could be fear of what we might witness or fear of loss of control. This construct of a veil has existed for so long that some might take issue with my premise, but perhaps not those of you who always see spirits around. For me, the veil is not growing thinner; there simply is not one. However, I know that many people celebrate the seasons of the veil and absolutely do see spirits. They love this time of ritual, and I celebrate with them!

One important thing I believe cannot be stressed enough is that different cultures and religions have long-standing histories around some of these topics. Experience and belief vary from person to person, culture to culture, and religion to religion. In no way do I intend to disparage any cultural or religious beliefs. Actually, to the contrary, this book is based on an amalgamation of many cultures. When all is said and done, many cultures believe similar things regarding energy beings; they are just passed down as different traditions. We know the belief is not new, that the spirit realm exists, and that spirits interact with us. From Siberian shamans to Greek oracles, communication with spirits has occurred since the beginning of recorded history.

As you read this book, try to keep an open mind, and then take what appeals to you. Perhaps mull over some of the other ideas. Keep in mind that just as energy changes form, we also may perceive energy differently. Further, your perception of energy may not be the same now as it will be by the end of the book. You may shift energetically.

Clearly, I will have a perspective, but although I may mention teachings from particular groups, I assure you that as a spiritual person, I do not solely follow the rules of one particular *religious* group. Human constructs have limited me for much of my life, but they do not now. I believe in the love of Christ for all, not just for the select or few. I find much wisdom in Buddhism and Buddha, but I am not Buddhist. However, I firmly believe I can honor those traditions without appropriating them in any way.

My spiritual life is esoteric and very personal to me, and I am very grateful for the richness of diversity that we all seek and have the freedom to embrace. The vital thing to know about spirits is that they are closer to us than many realize; they will work with any of us, which is a beautiful thing. My hope is that we can learn to better understand the entire spiritual realm since we are one with it, and it is one with our physical realm.

KEY CONCEPTS TO CONSIDER

This book may be your first entrance into the world of spirits, or perhaps you have read widely in this area. Either way, I would like you to consider several concepts that set the stage for the rest of our time together. First, there is a discussion of the differences between planes, dimensions, and realms. Then, we will consider what spirits are, whether they have free will, and where the spirits of physical beings go when they *cross over* from this mortal plane. Finally, we will look at reincarnation and how it applies to the ideas of what spirits are. In each case, you might encounter ideas you have heard before. In addition, you will most likely be exposed to new ideas because I tend to see some of these concepts through a different lens.

WHAT ARE PLANES, DIMENSIONS, AND REALMS?

Plane, *dimension*, and *realm* are three words that are often used interchangeably. In actuality, they have very different, distinct meanings. For our purposes, I would ask you to envision an existential plane similar to how a plane is described in mathematics—linear and 2D (like a tabletop). It is basically a single level, state, or region of reality corresponding to a certain energetic being. A dimension (as in mathematics) adds a third spatial element (like a box). It could be an amalgamation of multiple planes of existence. Finally, think of a realm in terms of quantum physics' string theory of *hyperspace*, a region of reality comprised of multiple dimensions.

You can read more about planes, dimensions, and realms in the appendix, but for the purposes here, know that everything is energy and it all oscillates or vibrates. In other words, no matter what dimension, plane, or realm in which energy is moving, it is moving at a certain rate called frequency. Learning to adjust your frequency is how you will begin to interact with all the varying spirit beings around you.

WHAT IS A SPIRIT?

The word spirit conjures up different meanings to different people. It quickly becomes apparent when merely researching the origin of the word that spirit, like many words, has several connotations. This is because many were attempting to define that which they could not see. Spirit is the vital breath that gives life to a being. The spirit referred to is not the physical body, but that part of the being that most cannot see. It is also a debated topic regarding whether spirit and soul are one and the same or different. For our purposes, I have decided to leave you to your thoughts on the meaning of the soul compared to that of the spirit.

We will turn our attention to the life force, the breath, which is beyond a human form—the spirits that move among us. Some may be able to see these spirits, and some may be able to sense them, but just know they are there. While reading, you may form or validate opinions regarding the comparisons and contrasts between spirit and soul.

The broad nature of the term will be addressed and embraced because there are many types of spirits. In many circumstances, these spirits may be the same depending on the way people are prepared to see them and the culture surrounding the context of the spirit. Simply put, our life force or spirit is our essence. Most religions and cultures have their own definitions and perceptions of a spirit, and many may be similar.

WHAT ABOUT REINCARNATION?

The concept of incarnation and reincarnation is essential because we may not all come from similar viewpoints. It is necessary to understand why we are on this planet called Earth. What is the point, really? Asking this question is fundamental to reading and diving into the world of the spirits around us. Many believe we come to Earth to learn lessons. Some even think we come here because it is such a harsh and cruel planet. I take issue with that. I believe Earth is bountiful and beautiful. Some would then say that it is humans who are horrible. Well, I propose we all tend to be at a high or low frequency based on the duality that exists in every living thing. It comes down to the choices we make. All energy beings can make that choice based on the Law of Duality.

What about incarnation, then? Why do we come to Earth? We all may have different answers, but the most repeated is we come to grow and evolve as energy beings. With the implied belief, Earth seems to be a spiritual growth boot camp of sorts. While on Earth, we feel or believe the linear and three-dimensional nature of Earth. We are used to feeling boundless and timeless; now, we feel limited. The dense nature of our physical bodies weighs us down.

I believe we are here for a completely different reason. The universe exists to experience itself. Not everything is about lessons; it is about experiences. We are not here for some video game to see if we can get to the next level. We are all intermingling and dancing in a so-called spiritual ascension all the time. We choose where we reside and what energies we choose to interact with while here or in the so-called spiritual realm.

Get ready for an introduction to many of those energy beings. Then, you can decide which ones you want to invite into your cosmic dance of being. Whether you believe you have one physical lifetime or many life-times (reincarnation), at least a part of you is in a body on Earth at this time. All beings are multidimensional, including humans. The problem is not that we don't understand all the possibilities. The problem is that we have forgotten our multidimensional nature and have been disconnected from much of ourselves.

The variety of beings that walk among us all the time is truly amazing. From nature spirits to angels to extraterrestrials to giant beings main-taining the dimensions to the tiny beings in particles, there are beings everywhere. We have often mistaken different vibrations for different beings. We also mistake different vibrations for other realms, dimen-sions, or planes and claim there is some sort of veil between us.

WHAT ABOUT FREE WILL?

Most seem to agree that there is some sort of blueprint of your life laid out before you are born (incarnate). I often question this life blueprint that claims the major life happenings are decided by your higher self before incarnating but that there will be twists and turns to help you speed along the lessons. Throw in free will—your own ability to choose instead of having it decided for you—and that is where the balance comes into play. So, where does that leave you? Perhaps, instead, there is a rough draft of sorts of what you wanted to learn at Bootcamp Earth, but your free will lets you make choices along the way.

You will have to decide for yourself whether or not you believe there is a blueprint for life on Earth. I can, however, reassure you that you have free will to live your life on your terms. What I do believe, as does almost every central belief system, is that there is some sort of repercussion for your actions—you reap what you sow, do unto others as you would have them do unto you, the rule of three, or karma. This is important in decid-ing if you want to entertain varying energy beings that carry certain residual energy or karma with them.

Whatever the case, because of duality, the energies we will meet are divided into polarities such as joy and misery, love and hatred, and light and darkness. All energy beings can manifest at any aspect of this spectrum of beingness. In this way, all energy beings are vibrational shapeshifters. All energy beings have free will. They can change their vibration and none of this is good or bad. It is just a different vibration, but all energy can choose.

Remember, the point of existing is to have experiences, not always to learn lessons. However, we spend much of our time resisting the ride called life and miss most of our present moments while in such resistance. Our ego keeps us stuck in *when I—then I* thinking, telling us we will participate and be happy when we lose weight, get more money, or find a lover. If we can remind ourselves of the universal oneness of which we are all a part, and if reality exists as the universe experiencing itself, then we are all collectively experiencing this reality but potentially perceiving it differently due to our broadband frequency width.

WHAT DOES *CROSSING* REALLY MEAN?

To discuss the spirits among us, we really must address the age-old question without definite proof of an answer—where do spirits go when they cross? Even in that question, the word *cross* is somewhat problematic. Have the spirits crossed? What have they crossed? The River Styx of Greek lore? The veil that is referred to and accepted so readily? It will be emphasized in this book that life does not end when the body dies and that there is no veil.

We live on after our physical form dies. Even though we are so identified with our bodies, in some cases obsessively so, they do not make up the whole of who we are. Just because our bodies will die does not mean our consciousness dies with our body. Energy never goes away; it just changes form. So, do we just return to dust? Or does our spirit-self live on in another form? Might it also live in another dimension? What about another realm? First, we need to realize that consciousness is independent of space or time. Second, it can exist in multiple places at one time. An example of this is spirit guides or ascended masters that are omnipresent—they are not restricted by space or time.

Because these concepts are so complex for us to grasp, we just think of everything as linear. We are born, we live, we die, we cross, we reincarnate. But consciousness doesn't work that way. If it is simpler to think of it that way, then no harm, no foul. However, it is becoming more apparent that parallel and multiple universes can and do exist simultaneously. This means that there are a multitude of places our spirit could cross or migrate to after death. It also means that our spirits can hang around. Things are just not as fixed and linear as we tend to think. Everything is energy, and all energy is part of one quantum consciousness. Our consciousness lives on after our human death. It may be in a different form than we have ever imagined. But it lives on in the collective consciousness and as a unique particle making up the whole.

WHAT ABOUT POSITIVITY AND NEGATIVITY?

According to the Law of Relativity, there is no distinction without comparison.[1] In other words, how do we know we are tasting sweet food if we have never experienced sour? We have our moral codes, such as laws and personal ethics, as a moral compass. We know that not everyone agrees with these codes or moral compasses. Likewise, many spirits have their own ideas of what they consider acceptable. Your wrong might be their right. That is why it is imperative that you know yourself and your intentions when working with spirits. They are every bit as real as you are, and it is no game when you intentionally intermingle your energy with any spirit from human to angel to extraterrestrial. Do not assume they play by or adhere to your rules.

Throughout this book, you will discover that spirits are different from us because of a difference in the vibrational frequency of their energy. This is distinguishable from the idea of raising your vibration to ascend or evolve spiritually. One of the main differences is there are no value judgments assigned to spirit frequencies; however, we often place value judgments on our own frequencies. The point of this book is that you can align your higher-self frequency to that of any spirit with absolutely no judgment attached.

WHAT ABOUT GENDER OF SPIRITS?

While many spirits may have a distinctly traditional male or female vibe when they connect with you, the truth is energy is neither male

. . . .
1. "Law of Relativity," Law of Relativity - Laws of the Universe, weebly.com. https://lawsoftheuniverse.weebly.com/law-of-relativity.html, accessed November 20, 2021.

nor female. Throughout the book, there may be descriptions of energy beings that typically have been characterized as male or female; however, always know that spirits may appear to you in the way that best meets your needs at the moment. Feel free to modify the genders as you see fit so that you can begin to connect. Mainly keep in mind that all energy, including yours, has attributes of all genders.

WHAT YOU WILL FIND IN THIS BOOK

You will meet many types of spirits as you read. In each chapter, you will be given a real-life example of sensing a particular spirit. These real-life stories will tell of the spirit being in its dual nature (flip side). In other words, there will be an account of both a benevolent and malevolent encounter. Next, you will read how to identify the spirit and distinguish it from other energetic beings. Finally, you will be shown how to connect with any of the spirits discussed. Should you feel the need to protect or avoid any of the beings addressed, don't worry, you will become a pro at that also.

On the other hand, you will be encouraged to honor entities when that respect is due. According to Carl Jung's idea of the collective unconscious, we are already intimately connected to spirits. The collective unconscious is the part of your unconscious mind that holds the experiences, wisdom, and memories of everyone.[2] Remember this when we begin to discuss the connection and collaboration with the spirits Also, keep in mind that the connection is not made just in dark, creepy houses. In fact, nature is one of the most common places to connect with many spirits and tap into the third eye or intuition.

Although there is a section in each chapter dedicated to demystifying concepts around spirit beings, things to contemplate are sprinkled throughout the entire book. As you approach the book, keep in mind that we all come from different viewpoints, backgrounds, and experiences that contribute to our perceptions. Therefore, practices and lists are dispersed throughout the chapters to provide you more opportunities in that area or to quickly summarize important points.

Although many different types of practices are suggested in this book, crystals are recommended to help adjust your frequency to various spirits.

. . . .
2. "Collective Unconscious," Definition and Facts, britannica.com, britannica .com/science/collective-unconscious, accessed November 20, 2021.

Many people have asked me why I am so drawn to crystals since I teach on just about every modality of everything I sell in my stores (SoulTopia, LLC). Allow me to emphasize that this is not just for a new age reason or because I love crystals. The key to connecting with the spirits that are all around us is to tune into their frequencies.

Crystals are some of the most straightforward tools to help accomplish this. They have a fixed rate of oscillation or vibration, whereas spirits have individual, varying frequencies. Once you know the crystals that are on the same or similar frequency as that of the spirit you are trying to reach, you will entrain with that frequency. The crystal will tune you in to the radio channel of the spirit.

Speaking of tuning into the frequency of the spirits, please know that this is the way you will meet any type of spirit you want to encounter, and this is why you should not be too concerned about the ones you don't want to encounter. Although we will go into more detail in later chapters of this book, just realize that if you can hold the frequency of a spirit, then you can remain in contact with it. However, one thing that will jolt us out of a frequency with a spirit is fear. An exception to this might be if they want us to be afraid and that is their vibration. Most of the time it is not their intention—we are simply afraid of the unknown. In any case, it is best when dealing with spirits of any kind to set the intention that any interaction be for your highest and best good.

WHY BOTHER WITH SPIRITS?
I HAVE ENOUGH DRAMA

The fact that you picked up this book and are reading it implies you are curious about the spirits that linger in our earthly, mundane realm. You may have a desire to connect with these spirits, or perhaps you have already encountered spirits all around you. Whatever the case, you have probably experienced something you cannot explain at some point in your life. You might believe this was a spirit alongside you, or perhaps you shrugged it off as coincidence. There is a strong possibility you had a time when the hairs on your arms stood up, or you had a tingle at the back of your neck.

If you are familiar with instinctual knowing and pay attention to your intuition, you probably heeded these subtleties as signs or even warnings.

But have you lived a life acutely aware of the spirits that walk near or with you every day? Do you see the spirits or even sense them daily?

The primary reason to connect is that you are surrounded by spirits all the time, whether you realize it or not. It is often so crowded around you that it may feel suffocating. These spirits affect your life, so you might as well learn to interact with them healthily. By opening up to different energies at varying vibrations, you will not only experience more, but you will also shape and mold different perspectives of these experiences.

To tune into these spirits, you may need to adjust a part of yourself that you were taught or chose to ignore. It will require you to trust your intuitive knowingness, and it may feel like your imagination, but we were given that imagination for a reason. Many times, it is remembering more than imagining. Just allow yourself to take a psychic leap of faith. Don't try too hard; just relax and trust. Try to have a little fun along the way as you learn about all the spirits that interact with you.

1
Spirit Guides

Every night was the same; some memories remembered and some in the misty fog of my compartmentalized and detached brain. I was scared to go to my room—petrified of who or what energy I might encounter there. It began at a very young age and was forgotten in the same mist of time and worlds apart. The one constant, besides the fear, was the Woman of the Hall. Every night, for as long as I could remember, the woman would float down the hall.

The house I grew up in had a central hall that led to the bedrooms and a large living area. The hall had beautiful marble flooring with a crystal chandelier. It was a perfect setting for the Woman of the Hall. She was a mixture of what I now might describe as an angel, faery, and extraterrestrial. However, at the time, it never crossed my mind to distinguish all the spirits I encountered.

The Woman of the Hall was somewhat translucent, predominantly bluish white, but with all the colors of this world and others. She had long, flowing, beautiful hair. Every night as I attempted once again to brave the dark, she would float slowly down the hall, whispering my name over and over. It was not entirely singing, yet it was not quite talking. It became a lullaby for me that lasted even as I grew older.

The woman never came all the way into my bedroom that I knew of; she just lovingly guided me to the realm of sleep with her voice. She was one spirit I could trust. However, the woman never showed her flip side. You see, I came to know at a very young age that there were other forms of energy who chose to be unkind. They exhibited two sides of energy. The Woman of the Hall always exuded soothing love to me.

This spirit guide may have been my guardian angel, a faery, an ancestor, an extraterrestrial, or a hybrid of all. It never mattered to me. All that mattered was the comfort she provided. I have known that spirits move among us for as long as I can remember and in my bedroom I met different kinds of beings that showed other frequencies. Still, I always knew the woman was watching over me. She was my first spirit guide, and I will never forget her.

THE FLIP SIDE

However, as I said, my room also contained the opposite side of a guide—the flip side of spirit. I suffered horrible night terrors, sleepwalking, sleep paralysis, and migraines as a young girl. Yes, I was the freaky girl who would walk in her sleep and stand at the side of the bed staring at you. I did this well into adulthood and, when I was in my thirties, even woke up in my short nightgown climbing my neighbor's fence.

But back to the flip side guide. There was always a wispy figure in my room. The figure had a decidedly male presence, and it was extremely controlling. It was always watching me as I tried to fall asleep. There was a little powder room attached to my bedroom. I would sit at the vanity and look in the mirror, and the reflection of my face would shift into the form of a grotesque man looking back at me. I would hear the words *she is mine*.

About ten years ago, I had a reading from a psychic. She went into a bit of a trance, and then her eyes opened, and in the voice of the flip side spirit, she said *she is mine*. That guide attempted to control me every night of my childhood. Yet, I most certainly do not belong to that malevolent guide because I chose not to when I was young, and I continue to choose not to belong to it now. However, I do believe in low vibration spirits that will try to get me to follow them. I know without a doubt they are real, just as are the higher frequency spirits. It is all about what we choose to allow or choose to follow. We always have a choice regarding spirits.

I believe many true seers are those who have detached from their physical body for some reason and still do it knowingly or unknowingly. They pull out of their bodies, either because of a near-death experience or a severe trauma. I did this for both reasons. The near-death experience was twice that I know of, and the trauma was much more often.

One form of detaching from the physical body is through astral projection, which will be discussed in the last chapter. I have done this and many people—that I know to indeed be psychic—have a way of pulling out of their bodies and connecting with the astral dimension where many spirits dwell. It is right here with us, but just at a differing frequency. (No veil at all, although sometimes I wish there was!)

INTRODUCING

As you begin this book, decide where you want to vibrate. What spirits do you want to allow into your world? They are just waiting for you to ask—trust me when I tell you that they are *all* waiting for you to ask.

All of us can use a little help in our corner from time to time. You have spirit guides whether you believe in them or not. Since our reality is based on our beliefs and perceptions, you will probably find no evidence of guides in your life if you choose not to believe. In fact, because your thoughts create your reality, guides may not exist in your reality because of your disbelief. However, suppose you believe or allow your thoughts to shift to the possibility of spirit guides. In that case, you will begin to have an inner knowing about their presence in your life. This will lead to experiences that confirm their existence.

Spirit guides are energy beings that help assist, direct, steer, or show us the way. It helps to think of these helpers like bumper pads in a bowling alley. We are trying to reach a destination, but we may need some spiritual bumper pads along the way to steer us in the direction of that destination. Where or to whom the guides lead us varies. Ultimately, the guide is directing us to our higher selves, or to that part of ourselves that is possibly our soul self or super consciousness. In other words, that part of us that is not our ego or conscious self. At some point, we may choose to remove those bumper pads and not work with spirit guides. This may be for a short time or an extended time. The point is that we work with guides as we need them or want to work with them. The guides teach us to remember and trust our intuition, which is our higher self.

There are as many types of spirit guides as there are spirits—an infinite number. The reason there are so many different types of spirit guides is due to all our different perceptions. Those perceptions of the spirit guides will be how you connect to or describe the spirits you work with within your reality. However, there are specific categories that seem to be perceived by people consistently. Please note that spirit guide is an umbrella category. Although many of the following chapters will present many different beings, most of the various beings can, and do, serve as spirit guides.

11 EXAMPLES OF SPIRIT GUIDES

1. Deceased loved ones, recently departed relatives, or friends and ancient ancestors
2. Animal companions (both living and deceased)
3. Your past, future, or parallel self
4. An aspect of yourself in some other dimension
5. Your future descendants
6. Guardian angel, angel, or archangel
7. Elementals, such as faeries or trees
8. Spirit animals
9. Living humans
10. Ascended masters
11. Extraterrestrial beings

IDENTIFYING

Spirit guides can come in almost any form. Many people believe they are only ethereal beings, which are beings not in a bodily form. However, this is a misconception because spirit guides can manifest in a human form or some other form. They are not limited to a particular state. This is a difficult concept for humans to wrap their minds around because we want to put a specific set of parameters on spirit guides. For instance, a spirit guide might manifest as a human or an animal to walk alongside you while you are lost on a stretch of road. They are capable of turning their energetic state into that of solid matter. (Of course, they could also be in spirit form.)

The question then becomes, how do you know it is a spirit guide versus a living being? You may not right away. You may think back later and realize you interacted with one of your guides. That is why it is crucial to become aware of the spirits all around you all the time and to stop being surprised by them. Of course, many of your spirit guides will be in spirit form. You may begin to identify them by merely asking them to reveal themselves to you.

You can ask for specific guides to work with you. Do not let anyone tell you that you must wait for the guide to come to you. Even if you feel you have no intuitive abilities at all, I guarantee that you can identify a guide and connect with them. Again, you can do this totally on your own. You may have a relative or mentor who was always special to you that you often feel around but dismiss it as your imagination. Just remember, your imagination is a spirit guide's playground!

When attempting to identify your spirit guides, pay special attention to signs and synchronicities—those happenstances or occurrences that are just too kismet to be coincidences. Carl Jung first defined synchronicity in the 1920s as the *simultaneous occurrence of two meaningfully but not causally connected events.*[3] You may have a bird that appears to you every time you need an answer. This synchronicity will help you identify an animal guide. What about the tree that always catches your attention on your walk or runs? Even a name that comes on every time you turn on the radio. Spirit guides love to speak through songs and nature. Repetition will help validate this feeling of knowing you are hearing from your guides.

There is a difference between serendipity and synchronicity. Serendipity is when something good accidentally happens. Think of the times you are short on cash, and you look in a jacket pocket only to find a twenty-dollar bill. Synchronicity is not just a single occurrence. It is a string of meaningful symbolic events. You can always ask for a sign to help you identify your guide. The most important thing is that you notice the signs and realize it is your guide trying to communicate.

Another critical thing to remember is that in most cases, your guides will present themselves in a form you are comfortable with accepting. In other words, they may present themselves as a human with a human name, or if you are comfortable with your guide in the form of an animal, the guide may take that form. The point is that guides can take on different shapes to make you feel at ease. Remember, you also are an energy being or spark of energy in your original nonphysical form. The form your guide takes is what you need at that particular point and space in time.

You may also identify a guide by a dream you have. It may be apparent that an energetic being is trying to connect with you once you begin to pay attention to your dreams. The key is to be aware of your dreams and trust that guides will connect with you if you allow them to do so.

. . . .

3. C.G. Jung, *Synchronicity: An Acausal Connecting Principle*, From Vol. 8. of the Collected Works of C. G. Jung (Jung Extracts), (Princeton: Princeton University Press, November 14, 2010).

The exciting thing about all the ways mentioned to identify your guide is that identification is through your own efforts. Many people choose to consult a psychic to pinpoint their guides. While this can be effective, always remember that you do not need anyone else to tell you or validate what guides you work with in life. You can determine and choose this for yourself. If you decide to consult a psychic for a spirit guide reading, an excellent way to validate the information they give you is to ask your guide(s) for a sign. Your guides will oblige you, so remember that ultimately, the journey you embark upon with your personal guides is one you can take with or without validation from others.

An ascended master is a type of spirit guide that lived on Earth at some point but has finished their karmic journey and ascended from Earth. Their purpose is to work with you on specific spiritual or detailed matters. They achieved mastery in their field when they were on Earth and probably lived many lifetimes.

Sometimes they are archetypes such as Kali Ma. Archetypes are universal symbols and images that come from the collective unconscious, as proffered by Carl Jung. For example, as the Hindu goddess of death, destruction, time, change, transformation, and creation, Kali Ma represents an ideal example of duality because she is the goddess of creation as much as she is the goddess of destruction. Chapter 2 will cover ascended masters in more detail.

THE SOLFEGGIO FREQUENCIES

Dating back to ancient history, Solfeggio frequencies are specific sound tones that help foster varied aspects of mind and body health. Having an understood positive healing effect on DNA, these sounds were said to be the fundamental frequencies used in both Western Christianity and Eastern Indian religions, and also used in Gregorian and Sanskrit chants.[4] So powerful that they were seen as a major threat to the Catholic Church, Solfeggio frequencies were once banned from the public and masses by the Vatican for their consciousness-expanding effect for the listener and singer. These healing tones were rediscovered in the 1970s by researcher Dr. Joseph Puleo by using a mathematical numerical reduction to identify six measurable tones that bring the body back

. . . .
4. Dr. Leonard Horowitz, and Joseph Puleo, *Healing Codes for the Biological Apocalypse*, (Tetrahedron Media, LLC, June 16, 2021), pp. 58-61, also pp. 345-6.

into homeostasis and promote healing.[5] Solfeggio frequencies produce more positive effects on the body than other sounds or tones due to their harmony with the Schumann Resonance of 8 hertz (also known as the Earth's heartbeat). [6]

The Schumann resonances match to various levels of human brainwave states, hence, the Solfeggio frequencies aid not only in healing but in other benefits such as awakening intuition and creativity, interrupting negativity, speaking your truth, and connecting with your higher self.

Practice
Identifying Spirits Through
11 Solfeggio Frequencies

The following practice will help you tap into and connect with different types of spirit guides found throughout this book by listening to different frequencies. The tones are easily found on the internet, and you will find many additional frequencies as well. Once you determine a tone, begin to play that tone when you are trying to connect with that frequency. You can integrate the Solfeggio frequencies into any area you feel comfortable when broadening your frequency bandwidth. There are suggestions that have proven successful for me, but you might want to experiment with the frequencies.

You may be in a state of stillness or meditation, or you may be out in nature, for example, walking in the woods. Use the tones in the manner most conducive to the way in which you are trying to connect and the type of spirit with which you are trying to connect.

111 Hertz[7]—Repeating Synchronicities
    Connect with angels and archangels

174 Hertz—Removes Pain, Serves as Anesthesia, and Clears Karmic Residue
    Connect with ancestors and loved ones

285 Hertz—Influences Energy Field, Heals Tissue, Serves as Blueprint for Health
    Connect with thought forms, demons, and predatory spirits

. . . .

5. Ibid.
6. Ibid.
7. Ibid.

396 Hertz—Liberates You of Fear and Guilt
Connect with ghosts, thought forms, demons, and predatory spirits

417 Hertz—Facilitates Change and Heals Trauma
Connect with land, place, or thing

432 Hertz—Miracle Tone of Nature
Connect with elementals and animal spirits

528 Hertz—Repairs DNA and Creates Miracles
Connect with multidimensional beings (extraterrestrials)

639 Hertz—Heals Relationships
Connect with animals, elementals, and loved ones

741 Hertz—Awakens Intuition
Connect with spirit guides, ascended masters, elementals, demons, and multidimensional beings (extraterrestrials)

852 Hertz—Attracts Soul Tribe
Connect with spirit guides, ancestors, loved ones, and multidimensional beings (extraterrestrials)

963 Hertz—Connects with Light and Spirit
Connect with angels, multidimensional beings (extraterrestrials), and those through astral travel, in parallel universes, and doppelgangers

CONNECTING

Assuming you have identified a spirit guide you want to get to know better, the best way to begin to connect with your spirit guide is to simply think of them. It sounds simple because it is. Remember that your guide is always accessible to you, but often you are unaware of its presence. However, when you consciously think of your guide, it is an invitation to them for more direct communication. They are always ready and willing to assist you; you only have to ask.

Another way to connect with your guides is to still your mind through meditation. Let's pause right here for a moment. The word meditation has many different connotations for different people, and some people even get territorial about the word. Others may experience resistance to the idea of doing it. Yes, it is an ancient tradition practiced worldwide by all different types of cultures. Still, there are a lot of misconceptions surrounding it.

Meditation in the context of this book is simply calming and quieting your mind in some form or fashion. There are various types of meditation to choose from, including, but not limited, to mindfulness, spiritual prayers or affirmations, attention to your breath, focused movement, mantras, transcendental, body scan meditation, and visualization. When attempting any of these methods, you may find it helpful to dim the lights or light a candle. You may want to play music or go outside in nature.

I have included some practices in this chapter that may be helpful and assist you in discovering a type of meditation that works well for you. However, the most crucial point I want to make here is how invaluable a tool meditation can be in your efforts to learn how to connect to spirit guides. I encourage you to find a technique that works well for you in quieting your mind and silencing any chaotic thoughts. Hopefully, you will find something you enjoy during your meditation time. Enjoyment will help you to establish a consistent practice as nothing will be more helpful to you in connecting to Spirit.

You may find that one of the easiest times to connect to spirit guides is when you start to get sleepy. This is because your mind is beginning to quiet on its own. You become less resistant to the thoughts that are, in fact, messages from your spirit guides that start drifting into your mind. If this happens to you and the spirit feels benevolent and non-threatening, go with it.

Notice if any particular clair is triggered. Clairs include clairvoyance (clear seeing), clairaudience (clear hearing), clairsentience (clear feeling), clairgustance (clear tasting), clairolfactory (clear smelling), clairtangency (clear touching), or claircognizance (clear knowing). (For more information about *clairs*, see the appendix.) For example, do you see anything? These can be shapes or symbols in your mind's eye, not necessarily something you can see with your physical vision. Take note of any thoughts you have. Notice any smells or physical sensations you experience. Any of these can be an indication that your guide is attempting to communicate with you. Don't dismiss these experiences; pay attention to them instead.

The critical thing to know is that guides *will* connect with you and often do; you are just unaware of it because you are not accepting subtle signs and synchronicities in your life as communication from a guide.

While you may expect to see your guide with your physical eyes, it is much more common to sense them or see them with your inner (or third) eye. You might hope to hear an audible voice when most of the time it is an inner knowing or sensing of a thought or a voice. Some guides, just like people or animals, are subtle, and some are bombastic. It depends on the personality and approach of the guide. Remember to ask to connect. It also helps if you have a sense of what type of guide you want to help you. Remember that you can choose them.

Crystals are some of the best tools to connect with any spirit because crystals have a fixed rate at which they vibrate. If you work with a crystal whose fixed vibrational frequency is close to that of the spirit with which you wish to connect, then the process will go much more smoothly because you will entrain to the crystal, which will help you entrain to the vibration of the spirit.

Some of the best crystals to connect with spirit guides, in general, are clear quartz, lapis lazuli, and amethyst. However, as you determine what type of guide you want to call upon, specific crystals can be utilized and are referred to throughout this book. Think of clear quartz as the voice of spirit, lapis lazuli as the bridge to spirit, and amethyst as the mind of spirit. You can hold them while meditating or trying to connect with your guide. You can also use an object that reminds you of your spirit guide to communicate with them. Other ways to connect with spirit guides are to journal about them, communicate through dreams, and ask for and anticipate signs.

Practice
Using Clairs to Connect

The following practices will help you connect with guides. The first practices will help you utilize your intuition as you begin to sense and realize the spirit world and physical world are only separated by vibrations. Your intuition in the form of clairs (clear sensing) will help you get in touch with these vibrations. When using your intuition, you may use clairvoyance (clear seeing), clairaudience (clear hearing), clairsentience (clear feeling), clairgustance (clear tasting), clairolfactory (clear smelling), clairtangency (clear touching), or claircognizance (clear knowing). While there are more clairs, these are the most utilized and will help you sense different vibrations and spirits around you. Again, you can read more about the clairs in the appendix.

Relax and put your feet on the ground to Mother Earth. Raise your crown up to the heavens. Call on your angels, guides, and ascended masters to join you in this meditation. Only those beings that you desire to join you are invited on your journey.

Become aware of your breathing. Breathe in to the count of four. Breathe out to the count of four. Breathe in to the count of four. Breathe out. Breathe in. Breathe out.

You are on a path. It is a path of your own making. Begin to walk down the path. Notice your surroundings as you walk. What do you see? Now you come to a clearing, and you see a bench in a garden. You walk over to the bench, and you sit down. You begin to notice the surroundings of the garden. What do you see? What do you smell? Then you notice a fruit tree in the garden. You walk up to the tree. You see beautiful fruit on the tree. What do you see? What do you smell? What do you taste? Then you notice animals and birds in the garden. They are happy you are in the garden, and they approach you without any fear. What do you see? What do you smell? What do you taste? What do you hear?

Now you realize it is time to return home. As you begin to leave, you see something on the bench. You know it is a gift just for you. Don't question it. Walk over and pick it up. If it is wrapped, unwrap it now. Know that the gift is yours for encouragement on your path back home and in your physical world. What do you see? What do you smell? What do you taste? What do you hear? What do you feel?

Now return to your path. As you walk the path, begin to return to your normal breathing. Bring your awareness back to your physical body. When you are ready—open your eyes.

Practice
11 Steps to Broaden Your Frequency Bandwidth

The following practice will help you know how to adjust your frequency so that you can connect to any type of spirit discussed in this book.

Everything is energy and vibrates at a different frequency. The range of frequencies we can connect with is our bandwidth. This practice is useful every time you want to connect with an energy of a different frequency. Broadening your bandwidth will help you connect with different types of frequencies, which means you will be able to connect and interact with different kinds of spirits. Throughout this book, there will be times when you are prompted to adjust your frequency; these are the steps you want to take.

Please do not ever become frustrated if you cannot alter your frequency. I am often asked why we have different frequencies and why some people seem better than others to connect with spirits. I firmly believe that while we all can connect, some of us tend to do so because certain events in our lives have led us to detach more easily, which helps us separate from our physical bodies and sense more frequencies. Many times, a traumatic event, be it emotional or physical, initially caused this tendency to detach. This is not to say that you needed to have a precipitating trauma to increase your bandwidth now, but I do opine this is the case in many instances.

You can integrate the Solfeggio frequencies into any area you feel comfortable when broadening your frequency bandwidth. Experiment with what works best for you.

1. Know some general guidelines ahead of time.
   Humans typically have fairly dense energy, which many will call a low vibration. This often is considered negative energy (although that is a much too simplistic judgment of energy). Some humans will work to raise their vibration. This is thought to be a more positive vibration, and many writers have placed their own value judgments into how to do this. Some will say to only listen to certain kinds of music. Although this has become generally accepted rhetoric, it is actually quite naïve. Music that will raise the vibration of one human may lower the vibration of another because emotions connected with music are a very personal matter.

   All the spirit beings discussed in this book have the capability of varying frequencies. Still, generally speaking, you can get an idea of the vibration of spirit beings and the frequency by tapping into how you feel. Do you feel anxiety, fear, or apprehension when you begin to think about a particular entity? If so, there is a good chance that it is not in alignment with your vibration.

You really do not need to assign a judgment to it. You can just make a note of how it makes you feel. If you feel lighter, joyful, or uplifted when thinking of another entity, perhaps it is a spirit that is more in alignment with you or what you may need at this time. Again, there is really no reason to assign negative or positive because it is energy vibrating at a particular frequency.

2. Figure out what frequency you currently want to connect with.
   You can use this book as a guide to help but realize that every category of beings has both *low and high vibrations*. This is perhaps a new concept because most teachings will categorize all angels, for example, as a higher frequency than humans. However, while they may be at a higher frequency than humans, every angel will have a distinct frequency and a particular frequency at different times. In other words, they have what we will refer to as flip sides. Nevertheless, get a general idea of what you want to connect with and the frequency of that being.

3. Quiet your mind and set the mood.
   Perhaps go to an area that will help you set the mood for the energy you are attempting to align with energetically. This will help you adjust your frequency. If you want to connect with elementals or nature, then it will be helpful to get outside. You can also surround yourself with items associated with the attributes of that energy.

4. Increase the noise to overcome the noise.
   In many cases, it helps to put on noise-canceling headphones or play loud sounds such as loud music to drown out the noises coming at you. Other frequencies may be subtle, or they may be extremely loud. If the noises feel like they are all talking or screaming at once, try flushing them out instead of drowning them out. The idea is to open up to all the waves of noise instead of trying to get quiet. In this way, you will flush out the one you want to hear. Then, it will suddenly become apparent among all the other cacophony.

5. If you need to lower your frequency (for example, to connect to a tree, which YES, is an energy being and can serve as a guide), embrace the density.

Try getting your feet in the soil and as close to nature as possible. Becoming really grounded will help you connect more with your dense energy. Remember, this is not about becoming negative; this is about a different frequency. It is slower, denser energy. It may feel heavy. Allow yourself to feel the fatigue, if necessary, from the denser energy. You may eat heavier foods or foods that come directly from the ground to help you feel a lower frequency.

6. If you need to raise your frequency, imagine leaving heaviness. Imagine yourself feeling lighter and free of the heaviness of this world. Contrary to what many have told you, raising your vibration does not mean you are a better person. This is just a different energy frequency. It will seem to flutter and may make you feel a little dizzy. Try closing your eyes and then barely opening them. You can even gaze into a candle to help you achieve this shift in vibration and frequency.

7. Ask the energy to meet you in the middle. You can try asking the spirit to meet you in the middle. For instance, they may lower their frequency while you raise yours or vice versa. This may expedite the process if the spirit agrees to such an arrangement.

8. Learn to focus your attention with concentrated intentionality. In other words, it's one thing to decide what you are trying to connect to, but focusing with purpose is also necessary.

9. Expect to connect; expect to broaden your bandwidth. Tell yourself you will sense and see other frequencies. Be patient and practice.

10. Tune into the variety of your bandwidth regularly to maintain your ease of contact.

11. Focus on the world of frequency and vibration instead of the dense, earthly world.

PROTECTING

Always remember—you have free will. You can choose not to work with a guide just as easily as you can choose to work with one. In fact, you can specify the exact parameters of how a spirit is allowed to work with you, and I highly encourage you to do just that! It is my opinion that it is critical to set an intention before connecting to any energy, being that they are only allowed to interact with or work with you if it is for your highest and best good. This is particularly important if you deliberately choose to work with any lower vibrational beings. However, I advise you do this even if you believe yourself to be working with a high vibrational archangel. There is always the possibility that you may not be as adept at identifying energy as you think you are, and high vibration does not necessarily always equate to benevolence. It is always better to be safe than sorry!

If the vibe of a guide makes you feel uncomfortable, you might want to avoid that guide. Think of it this way—guides are here to help lead you to a purpose. If they are not directing you to something that you believe is beneficial in your life, then perhaps you should not work with them. It is much like a human leader or partner. If you are not sure, look for red flags. In general, a guide does not expect to be worshipped and is not possessive; a guide will never tell you to only listen to them and obey them. They will not become threatened by you seeking other counsel because they only have your best interest in mind. They typically will not present themselves as scary or angry. They will not judge you or demand things from you. They guide and suggest. Yet some will be more forceful than others in personality. However, if it ever feels close to an abusive relationship, it is not the guide for you. You do not have to work with guides who do not honor your ability to choose.

Many will tell you that you should only work with guides of pure light. Due to the Law of Duality[8], which states that all energy encompasses both ends of the spectrum— light and dark, negative and positive, good and evil, and everything in between—this cannot be true. Remember, because of duality, energies are divided into polarities such as joy and misery, love and hatred, and light and darkness. All energy has the capability of different sides of the coin. They really should not be judged. It is just energy—as above, so below.

Further, there may be times you choose to work with a neutral or lower vibration guide for various reasons, for example, shadow work. Shadow work is work on that part of ourselves that we hide from others

. . . .
8. "The Spiritual Law of Duality," thesoulmedic.com, https://www.thesoul medic.com/the-spiritual-law-of-duality/, accessed November 20, 2021

and sometimes even from ourselves. A lower vibration guide may help you navigate some of your shadow work.

For instance, a lower vibration guide may help you find your voice when you lack the self-confidence to stand up for yourself or don't know what to say in a given situation. Suppose you feel disempowered or taken advantage of by another person. In that case, a lower vibration guide may give you the strength to confront the other person.

Be aware that this lower vibration guide may not filter words the way a higher vibration guide would, but perhaps there are times when you need to just let the words flow and state your truth. Once the guide helps you find the courage to face your fears, speak your truth, and stand up for yourself, you may not need to work with that guide anymore.

Practice
11 Spirit Guide Red Flags

Following are eleven red flags to look for when working with spirit guides. However, as you work with lower frequency guides, you may tolerate some of these attributes in a spirit guide because of the work you are doing with that being. Use this list to become aware of how different energies in spirit treat you just as you would energies or people in physical form.

1. A guide that distracts you from the purpose for which you needed their guidance.
2. A guide that causes unnecessary chaos in your life.
3. A judgmental guide that seems to criticize you rather than uplift you.
4. A guide that seeks only worship.
5. A guide that gets possessive or jealous.
6. A guide that is abusive.
7. A guide that refuses to ever let you get to know them.
8. A guide that makes you feel uncomfortable in a sexual way.
9. A guide that seems to zap you of your energy.
10. A guide that entices you to do things you do not want to do.
11. A guide that scares you.

COLLABORATING

Spirit guides are all about collaboration. This really is their purpose. Always keep in mind that they are guiding you; they are suggesting, not commanding. The rudder of the ship is not the captain of the ship, nor is it the ship. Since guides do have your highest good in mind, they help you, but they don't tell you; they point you to your higher self and Source, or whatever you believe is your destiny. A spirit guide can help you with any area of your life by teaching, advising, and encouraging in broad terms or specifics—projects, work, romance, health, or adventure. Spirit guides also love to work in beautiful ways by giving you a nudge to interact with someone else.

An example of collaborating with spirit guides is when you are in a dispute with someone and cannot seem to resolve it. You can get your spirit guide to serve as a mediator and approach the spirit guide of the other party to the dispute. This works exceptionally well with guardian angels or the guide that is always with the person. Simply ask your guide to visit the other person's guide and ask them to reconsider their position. Know that your guide will probably come back to you with anything you need to consider adjusting in your own behavior. This really works! Getting one spirit guide to talk to another will save you lots of money and heartbreak in serious situations, so make sure to start practicing as soon as possible.

Another way your guides collaborate with you is by giving you energetic nudges to help someone else. Spirit guides also alert you to danger, comfort you in sorrow, and rejoice with you in victory. Like friends, you want guides who have your back and work for your highest and best good. As you learn to work with your guides, you will become more and more particular about which guides you work with in life.

HONORING

It is a good idea to always honor your spirit guides. There are different ways to honor them depending on the guide. If it is a grandmother, you might want to wear her favorite perfume or place her favorite flower in a vase. If it is an animal, you may want to wear a token to symbolize them. You can set up a sacred space or altar in your house to pay honor to your spirit guides if you wish. You can place photos, candles, memorabilia, statues, or anything you believe will honor your guide. This is not about worshipping your guide, unless you have a guide in a culture where you think it is necessary.

As with everything, it is always good to express gratitude to your spirit guides for their help. Just as we like to be acknowledged and appreciated when we help someone, guides are also more likely to work with you if you recognize and thank them for their assistance.

It is beneficial, and interesting, to keep a spirit guide journal. Begin to write down everything you know about your different guides and how they interact with you. Not only will this document your experiences, it will also help to increase your confidence that your guide is indeed assisting you. This may be helpful any time doubt creeps in. Also, it is yet another way to acknowledge and honor them.

DEMYSTIFYING

There are many unnecessary rules, limitations, and misconceptions surrounding spirit guides. Remember that everything and everyone is energy, including you. So, in theory, you could be a spirit guide. Many will balk at this and tell you that you must need to pass on to be a spirit guide. No, you do not. We are all spirits of some form.

When first connecting with a guide, you may hear that you must say a prayer before you try to connect. Well, what if you don't pray? Does this mean you cannot connect with a spirit guide? Of course not. If you want to pray, then pray. If you are going to set an intention to meet a specific type of guide, then set an intention.

There is also a lot of cryptic talk around the fact that you should never play with a Ouija board, including to find out a spirit guide's name. This is the stuff of Hollywood. Do Ouija boards potentially have a lot of collective energetic fear connected to them? Perhaps they do, but if you want to use a Ouija board or a pendulum with a board that has letters, then go right ahead. The fear you assign to it is the power you give it.

Another misconception is that if a guide does not tell you their name, you should not work with them. Often a guide does not tell you their name right away because it may be a name you cannot even pronounce. They also may not initially tell you their name because you have preconceptions about who they represent. Ask for another name or make up a name to call them. This fear, that if a guide will not tell you its name it is a bad omen, perhaps stems from exorcisms where alleged demons will not say their names. (It is believed by some that if you can get a demon to say its name, then you will have power over it.)

Speaking of lower vibrations, many will claim you should never have a lower vibration being as a guide. While not everyone is suited to work with a lower vibration guide, some of you may be called to work in the shadow realms and you may work with a lower vibration guide. (An example was given in this chapter under "Protecting.") Remember, this guide also has duality and can choose to resonate at a higher vibration. It is worth repeating that a guide working for your highest good will not tell you what to do. They will make suggestions but not demands, and they will not judge you.

We will address angels later, but many people will tell you they are not guides. Well, of course, an angel can be a guide. You will also hear that a guide is still cycling through their karma. There are many people who do not believe in karma, yet they still have guides.

You will often hear that we all have a spirit guide that incarnates with us throughout our entire lifetime. However, something to consider is whether that is truly a guide or perhaps some other aspect/version of yourself—maybe your higher self. (After all, who knows you better?)

2
Ascended Masters

Years ago, I was giving a reading over the phone to a client I had never met. She insisted on getting a reading with me and, even though I was on vacation, I conceded. I felt an urgency and a pushiness, but it did not feel it was coming from her. I knew to listen to whatever spirit was impressing this on me.

Just as the reading began, I felt quite uncomfortable because the client was speaking about a relationship and I blurted out, *they will feel my wrath if this discrimination does not stop!* I then asked her *who is your friend Oya? She is about to tear apart your workplace.* The extremely professional and dignified client told me she did not have a friend named Oya, but she was indeed being discriminated against in her job.

I managed to get information on Oya (with whom I am now very familiar) and told my client that Oya is a fierce Yoruba Orisha. I have categorized her here as an ascended master because she was serving a specific purpose for the client as ascended masters often do. Please recall that spirit guides are a broad umbrella category that many beings may fall into. The important thing is that we connect with them. At that time, my client just wanted answers and Oya was working on her behalf. I emphasized that she needed to look up Oya and begin to talk to her because she would help. Of course she did, and we both learned so much more about the powerful Orisha Oya.

THE FLIP SIDE

I see many people who are in abusive relationships. I am not a counselor but have been involved in a women's shelter for more than half my life. The ascended master that helps those who have been abused is Kali. You may wonder why I have her on the flip side. Kali, just like Oya, will help those in need, but beware to those who get in their way. Their sense of justice does involve revenge. They will serve as judge and jury. I know this from my own life.

INTRODUCING

An ascended master is a spirit being who has evolved out of the need for a physical form. Ascend means to move upward and master means one who is skilled. Therefore, ascended masters are those who were skilled and rose out of the need for a physical body. At one time, most ascended masters had many lives in a physical body, but it is thought that they have cycled through or completed their karma and therefore have no need to reincarnate.

It is important to note that we have both our ego-driven selves (care mainly about earthly matters) and our higher conscious selves (realize there is more to our existence than merely the day-to-day Earth issues). I sometimes refer to the higher conscious simply as the higher self—some might call it the soul. So, ascension is not necessarily rising up into heaven, for example, but merging with our higher selves.

It is also important to keep in mind that ascended masters are not the past-life person. In other words, it is not the ego self that ascended, it is the higher self. So, when you call on an ascended master, it is the higher self that responds, not their former life or lives persona.

There are countless ascended masters; some are from ancient times and some from recent times. Some are archetypes or represent the characteristics that reside in all our collective unconscious. Archetypes are actually thought forms (as described in chapter 9) fed by individual and collective consciousness making them extremely powerful spirit beings.

Regardless of who they were in their countless past lives, they return as a special type of guide to help us in all areas of life. They will help us in spiritual matters, but they will also help us in other areas such as relationships or work. These spirit beings are not bound by space or time and are available to help us when we call on them.

Much of the ways to connect and collaborate with them is similar to what was described in chapter 1 regarding spirits guides and to archangels in chapter 3. The biggest difference is that they have lived through and experienced what we experience as humans. Many also learned from or may in fact be multidimensionals (extraterrestrials) as described in chapter 10. Although ascended masters are often associated with certain religions, you do not have to be religious to call on any of these spiritual beings.

IDENTIFYING

Ascended masters typically have extremely high vibrations. Let's pause a moment here—high vibration in this sense does not mean they are necessarily what you or I would consider perfect beings. After all, who makes that determination? This high vibration is one of frequency, not value. However, the most popular ascended masters are spirit beings with both types of high vibration. Following is a short list of some ascended masters. This list is in no way meant to be all-inclusive.

- **Buddha** lived the extremes of life on Earth. He was born a rich prince but chose life as a hermit in order to gain enlightenment. He opined the key to happiness was to live a life of moderation in all things. He taught that happiness comes from inner peace achieved through meditation.
- **Jesus** lived a life of compassion and taught forgiveness. He performed many miracles and taught his followers to always love those who seemed unlovable.
- **Mary Magdalene** was a faithful follower and a strong leader and teacher. She was misjudged but held her head high nonetheless.
- **Kali** is a goddess that is the perfect representation of the duality in all. She lovingly helps us face our shadows and fears but will destroy anything that will keep us in bondage.
- **Quan Yin** is a Chinese goddess of compassion and mercy. She cared so much for humankind that after her enlightenment she chose to remain in her physical human form instead of ascending to Buddhahood.
- **Lakshmi** is a beautiful Hindu goddess of prosperity and good fortune.
- **Devi** is a Hindu goddess who is believed to be the female energy of God. She is a goddess of duality. She protects her villagers but notably slayed a buffalo demon.
- **Krishna**, the Divine Lover, is worshipped as the eighth incarnation of Vishnu, one of the three Gods in the Hindu trinity. His love is eternal, infinite, and boundless.
- **Mother Mary or Our Lady of Guadalupe** is the mother of Jesus and represents mothering energy. She is loving, nurturing, and merciful.

- **Merlin** is a wizard who guided King Arthur. He helps us know that we are all alchemists and have the ability to transmute (change) the form of energy.
- **Oya** is all about change, release, and empowerment. She comes into our lives to help us know that we all possess the power to change even when we are resistant to it. Be aware that she is fierce and will bring about the chaos needed for transformation if we call upon her and do not do the necessary work.
- **Tesla** helps us claim our genius and recharge our own spark when we feel we are underappreciated or go unnoticed.
- **Walt Disney** was a future-focused innovator and entrepreneur in the entertainment and engineering fields. He used imagination and creativity to pioneer animation and color for television and animatronics for his theme parks. Disney knew that the only way to keep up with the changing times was to work tirelessly and never rest on his laurels or the future would beat him to tomorrow.

CONNECTING

Connecting with an ascended master is much the same as connecting to any other type of spirit guide. It really isn't the connection that is different but the purpose of connecting. Using the examples from the "Identifying" section in this chapter let's walk through a few purposes to connect with these ascended masters.

- **Buddha** helps you see the world through a broader lens. He helps you find joy, laughter, and inner peace. However, should you face suffering, you know that you are learning tolerance, compassion, and acceptance.
- **Jesus** helps you forgive yourself and others. The Christ consciousness is one of deep love and compassion for all. He can also help you with manifestation and healing.
- **Mary Magdalene** can help you to stay the course when you feel misjudged. She also will help you learn independence.

- **Kali** helps you find your own sense of courage and determination. She will help you when you are facing seemingly insurmountable challenges.

- **Quan Yin** helps you find compassion for yourself and others. She will help nurture you through difficult times, supporting you in knowing you are worthy to give and receive love. She also helps with with motherhood and aids children when they need assistance. Quan Yin's energy reminds me of Archangel Haniel whom you will meet in the next chapter.

- **Lakshmi** is perfect to help you in matters of beauty and prosperity. She helps you with your home. If you feel overwhelmed with home chores, call on Lakshmi for assistance. She reminds me of Archangel Jophiel whom you will meet in the next chapter.

- **Devi** is the ascended master to call on for two primary areas. First, call on her if you need help in your career. Second, call on her for purification when your body is exhausted.

- **Krishna** is ready to help with romantic relationships. Call on him for help in any relationship but do so with the anticipation of happiness and joy.

- **Mother Mary or Our Lady of Guadalupe** is ready to help you with any area regarding children, compassion, and forgiveness. Her gentleness is an overwhelming energy that will really help if you are in despair. She will help you with miracles and with healing.

- **Merlin** is ideal to help you with your magic, alchemy, or transmutation in whatever way you go about those things in your life—because we all do, just in different ways. Not only will he help you with your psychic abilities, but he will also help you time travel, shape-shift, and astral project. His energy is very much that of Archangel Raziel.

- **Oya** is ideal to call on when there are storms in your life, and you need a teacher to not only protect you but to help you learn to weather the storms yourself by becoming stronger.

- **Tesla** is perfect to help you in any area where you are attempting to advance innovation.

- **Walt Disney** will teach you how to make your dreams a reality when you have a dream that seems too good to be true.

Practice
11 Steps for Connecting
with an Ascended Master

The following practice will give you steps to connect to a specific ascended master to help with certain needs.

1. Remember that they are willing to work with you, but you can select whom you want to work with for any given issue at any given time.

2. Connect to your higher self. Realize that they see the overall soul-purpose perspective.

3. Decide what you are wanting assistance, guidance, or help with in your life.

4. Based on the help you need, you can now pick one of the ascended masters mentioned in this chapter. However, you can also work with many others not listed, such as ascended master elementals, ascended master animals, or with multidimensional galactic beings from chapter 10.

5. Once you know the ascended master you want to work with, familiarize yourself with the attributes and signs associated with that ascended master.

6. You want to familiarize yourself and set your intention of what you want before you call on an ascended master to know what to anticipate.

7. Based on the personality and characteristics of that ascended master, you will now know what to watch for when you call on them. This will help you connect with their frequency.

8. Now you are ready to call on the ascended master. It can be as simple as saying their name.

9. If you have the time, space, and circumstances, you may choose to do things to help you feel the presence of the ascended master,

such as lighting a candle that is the color associated with them or holding a crystal and saying the ascended master's name.

10. Still your mind and try to think of things associated with that ascended master.

11. Begin to sense the frequency change in not only your mind and body but also the environment and things around you.

PROTECTING

Historically, ascended masters are here to help us get in touch with our higher selves and ascend. But please know that this may also take place through shadow work, which may involve working with ascended masters that many may think would not have ascended according to judgments. However, it cannot bear repeating enough (because many of us confuse higher vibration and higher frequency) that there may be those ascended masters that are of duality. In fact, it is a definite—all energy has duality. Therefore, there may be a time to protect from some of the ascended masters you work with; although most of the time, they are the ones protecting you.

COLLABORATING

The very best way to collaborate with your ascended master is to listen to them. They are a teacher, a mentor, and a coach. They are willing to help you, but you must listen. The collaboration is not totally one sided, but it is one of teacher to student. You collaborate by taking their advice to help better your life and those around you.

HONORING

Many ascended masters are associated with religious or cultural beliefs. While you do not have to ascribe to these beliefs to connect with the ascended masters, you do want to pay honor and respect to the religion and culture when working with any of these ascended masters.

This book is not, nor was it intended to be, an encyclopedia of ascended masters. It is intended to let you know these spirit entities intermingle with us all the time. They are available to you. They can help you understand other energies. However, it is incumbent upon you to get to know ascended masters better by reading about them and researching them. Not only does it show honor and respect, but it will also help you become closer to the ascended master.

DEMYSTIFYING

The duality of spirits really shows up when dealing with ascended masters. Just because a spirit has ascended does not make it any less fierce and capable of warrior-like behavior. Who are we to know what is judged worthy to cycle out of karma? It is up to you to decide what type of teacher or mentor you want from an ascended master.

Further, ascended masters can be energies that were not human, such as animals, elementals, or galactic beings. Perhaps you will work with an ascended master that is a mosquito. This mosquito may teach you everything you need to know about tolerance. No, the mosquito was not a human, but why do we insist humans are above insects and animals?

Also remember that ascended masters do not have to have anything to do with spirituality. Perhaps they are to help us with a purpose such as proficiency at a job. This is why I included Tesla and Walt Disney as ascended masters. Ascending is about rising up in any way that is needed at a particular time in our lives. Another key point to consider is that you can ascend here on Earth. Let's stop waiting for some next level up. You are ready to level up now!

3

Angels and Archangels

As a young mother, I struggled to do my very best at everything, including trying to please everyone in my life. After graduating from law school at the age of twenty-four, I got married and had my first child. I attended a church that encouraged mothers to stay home and raise their children, yet I wanted to work. My ambivalence about not staying home with my child and pursuing a career triggered my old familiar nemesis—depression.

Depression had been part of my life for as long as I could remember, and seemed to rule it at times. That was the case then. Even though I attempted to keep a big smile on my face and had an impressive job, went to church, drove a fancy car, and had the ideal family—I was still plagued by overwhelming bouts of depression. Eventually, I started becoming very self-destructive until I finally voluntarily checked myself into a mental hospital.

When I first arrived there, at the height of 5'7", I weighed only 99 pounds. I was told that I was severely malnourished and perhaps only a month away from certain death. I felt like a complete failure. After all, my priority had always been to please all the people in my life, and now, even though I knew on some level that it had been an act of bravery to check myself into the hospital, I also felt I had let down everyone in my life and disappointed them in a significant way. Everything about me felt like an utter failure.

The first night I was in the hospital, a nondescript female patient walked up to me and said in a very comforting voice, *Hello, I am your angel. Remember me? You are going to be okay, and I will be with you the whole time. Just watch for my signs.* I thought to myself, *Oh great, here we go. This is going to be interesting.* But then the patient simply smiled and walked away. This was okay because I did not feel like talking and just wanted to be left alone. However, I couldn't help wondering why she had to be so cryptic. *Just tell me the darn sign if you really are some kind of an angel!*

I was on suicide watch the first few days at the hospital. Those days are still primarily a blur. However, I did keep an eye out for the so-called angel. Yet, she was nowhere to be found. *Well, so much for that!* I thought.

On the third day, I began to sit in on group sessions. I did not want to talk during group. Still, I did enjoy looking out the window, grateful for an opportunity to see outside. Every group session, I began to notice three squirrels and three blue jays outside the window. They all seemed to tease one another. Eventually, watching their silly antics, I finally began to smile—just a little. The group sessions were three times a day, every day. So, I would see the three squirrels and the three blue jays and smile three times every day.

About a week into my stay, I dreamed of the woman who had claimed to be an angel. It was a lucid dream, and I realized that the woman was an angel that had been with me for much of my life. The angel chose to appear to me in human form that first day to give me reassurance because, at that point, I had seemingly lost all hope. I realize now that the squirrels and the blue jays were probably little angels themselves.

THE FLIP SIDE

It is said that when God created the angels, the most beautiful angel of all was Lucifer, whose name means *light-bearer*. The story of the fall of Lucifer is told primarily in two books of the Christian Bible: Ezekiel and Isaiah. Lucifer thought he would be like the most high, so he was cast out of Heaven. However, when recounting the story of the fall of Lucifer, it is essential to emphasize the duality in all energy. There is no light without dark.

About three years ago, I was working in the office at one of my Soul-Topia metaphysical stores. I had no reason to go out onto the store floor that day, but for some reason I did. I saw a young man standing near the hall leading to my office. He seemed to radiate kindness, and yet something felt a little off. I looked around the store, and no one seemed to be helping him even though they were not busy. I asked him if he needed help, and he told me he was about to go on dialysis and wondered if there was a crystal that might help him.

It was at that point that I broke one of my own rules. I asked if I could give him energy. I typically will not do this because I do not want to make anyone feel uncomfortable. However, the young man immediately said yes. We stood right there in the store, and without touching him, I put my hand in the vicinity of his kidneys and began to pull the sickness out of him. It was then that I broke another one of my own rules. I took the energy on myself. I literally began thinking that I needed to help him no matter the cost to me.

The young man left the store, and I never saw him again. It has been three years since I took on that energy, and I have had chronic kidney issues ever since. When it occurred to me several months later that maybe I had taken on some of his energy, my husband and I reviewed the store's security tapes to see exactly what had happened that day. You can see me coming out to the floor on that day's video and then just standing there. There is no one else standing there with me. Still, you can partially see me holding my hands approximately where I would have while sending the man energy.

I have since wondered whether he was a benevolent or malevolent angel. I have finally reached the conclusion that the being was most likely an angel choosing to do the work of someone wanting to cause harm. Despite its friendly outward appearance, it intended me harm. Was it an angel choosing to walk the flip side, or was it a shape-shifting demon? I propose that it could have been either, for what seems negative to one person may seem positive to someone else. And, until it all plays out in the end, we can't really know with any certainty whether an experience was or wasn't ultimately for our highest good. There is no distinction without comparison.

Ultimately, the differences in these energies come down to the frequency of the vibration. Is it in alignment with what you are seeking to accomplish? If so, there are times when the so-called fallen angels, darker angels, or what some call demons might serve a purpose in your life that ultimately help you evolve. These beings are discussed in chapter 9.

INTRODUCING

Angels have interacted with humans since time began. In fact, most major religions can agree on very little, but all the worldwide religions with the most followers (Islam, Christianity, Buddhism, Judaism, and Hinduism) can agree upon the existence of angels. They may not agree on the angels' names or what they are sent to accomplish, but they all agree that angels exist.

The angels referred to in this chapter are energetic beings that are mostly believed to have never walked as humans but come directly from God or Source. The word *angel* means messenger of God. The *el* in angel means they are of God. Although undoubtedly many more exist, there are two exceptions that we know of: Sandalphon (Prophet Elijah) and Metatron (Prophet Enoch). Sandalphon's and Metatron's names do not end in *el* because they incarnated as men and later became angels.

Angels are said to love unconditionally with pure love. However, as you read in the flip side, angels can have a dual nature. Angels are universal archetypes that are not owned by any particular sect or religion. It is said that we all have at least one guardian angel. However, I suspect there are times when we are actually working with, being protected by, or guided by multiple angels all at the same time. We certainly can do so if we choose to. Conversely, there are probably times when we work with a particular angel only for a short time for a specific situation or purpose.

Angels are androgynous. They may have an energy that seems more traditionally feminine or masculine and may be referred to as one or the other. One way they differ from some spirit guides is that they are often believed to have no ego. They also will not typically interfere with our free will. However, I do think angels themselves have free will and can and do make choices. They are just not known for pushing those choices on us. Further, just like most spirit guides, angels do not want us to worship them.

Archangels are mightier angels that represent the characteristics of God or Source. The Greek *arche* means ruler, and *angelos* means messenger. Archangels are omnipresent, meaning they can be in more than one place at a time. They expect us to exercise our free will and call on them when we need them and will not typically intervene in our matters unless we ask them to. However, there are occasions when they do intervene, such as in natural disasters or other disasters such as fires and accidents, whether we call on them or not.

IDENTIFYING

There are an infinite number of angels and simply no way in the context of this book to go through them individually regarding how to identify them. Instead, we will discuss some ways to identify angels in general.

Angels are often identified by the way they communicate through signs, synchronicities, and songs. If you begin to see the repetitive numbers 111 or 222, there is a good chance an angel is trying to get your attention. Although angels may not always have wings as we tend to think of them, they tend to send feathers as a sign since we have associated wings with angels for so long. Remember that energy beings that serve as guides will often appear to us as we expect to see them. A lot of this expectation comes from religious teachings that have been adopted and folded into spiritual teachings.

Angels will often call out your name in your inner mind. If you hear your name and no one is around, this is often an angelic being communicating with you. Celestial beings will also come to you in dreams, cloud formations, and animal signs.

A significant way angels communicate with you is through music. You might hear a song with the word angel in it or a song with lyrics that seem to provide the answer to a question you were just thinking about when the music began to play. You might hear the favorite song of a loved one come on the radio, or your playlist may play something in random order.

Ashlie, whom you will meet later in this book, tells how her brother who sadly died by suicide, communicated several times. Ashlie listened to a heavy metal playlist while sitting in a spa shortly after her brother's funeral. The playlist contained no country music, but suddenly, her brother's favorite Tim McGraw song started playing. It also just happened to be the song that was played at his funeral. Ashlie knows that not only were angels with her, but her brother was communicating with her through music.

There are also many archangels, so we will go through some of the major ones and how to identify them. While we may refer to archangels as male or female due to their distinctive masculine or feminine energy, it is important to note that they are all androgynous. We will also mention aura colors associated with archangels because the color might help us identify which archangel we are working with at any given time or suggest colors of crystals or candles we might want to use to connect with them.

A Few Significant Archangels

Archangel Ariel means *lioness of God*. She is the archangel of animals, plants, the environment, and your physical needs. Her aura is a pale pink. Suppose you see or dream about lions, sense wind in your hair, or feel a sudden compassion rush over you about an animal or the environment. In that case, you are probably working with Archangel Ariel. When trying to shift your frequency to connect to animals, plants, the environment, or any elementals, Ariel is one of your most essential helpers.

Archangel Azrael is another important archangel. His name means *whom God helps*. He gets a nasty rap as the angel of death, but he does not look like the grim reaper at all. He wears no dark hood and carries no sickle. He actually has an off-white to creamy pale-yellow aura, and his energy is highly compassionate and respectful. He does not decide who is dying. Instead, he comforts those who are dying and those who are grieving. He also helps lead those who are transitioning to the light. You can identify Azrael by his respect and compassion. If you are grieving for a loved one because they have passed or are ill, call on Archangel Azrael. Also, contact Azrael if you are sick and fearful of physical death. Ministers, counselors, first responders, and hospice workers can all benefit by working with Archangel Azrael.

Archangel Chamuel means *he who sees God*. He has a pale green aura and feels very down to earth. The feeling is almost like someone you would just want to hang out with as a friend. You might sense a tingly feeling when you first feel him, but it settles down very quickly. Anytime you have lost something, call on Chamuel—from small things like keys to essential things like life purpose. Instead of cussing when you can't find your keys, try saying, *Chamuel, where are my keys*. It works! He also helps with other things lost, like world peace or our own inner peace. That is why he can also help with any stress or anxiety you may encounter.

Archangel Gabriel is known as the guardian of the west, water, and autumn. Many times, he is referred to as Gabriella. His name means *messenger of God, or God is my strength*. He brought the message of the coming of Christ to the Virgin Mary and the birth of John the Baptist to Elizabeth. Known as Gibrail to the Muslims, Gibrail was also said to have delivered and dictated the Quran to Mohammed at Mount Hira. His energy is relatively easily identified by several factors. First, his aura is copper, just like the trumpet he carries. Because of this, he is said to be around when you find a penny, because they used to be made out of copper (now they only have a copper coating). He is also known to carry a copper chalice. He will get his message across to you because he is an archangel of action. Finally, Gabriel is the messenger angel. He is great to call on when attempting to shift your vibration to communicate between planes.

Archangel Haniel is identified by feminine energy. Her name means the *grace of God*. She has a bluish-white aura and is associated with the moon and goddess energy. She is poised, patient, mystical, and graceful. Her energy feels quite regal. She will help you with your clairvoyance (clear seeing or intuition) and help you find your purpose in life. She also clears away heartbreak.

Archangel Jeremiel typically has masculine energy with a violet aura. His name means *the mercy of God*. He is exceptionally patient and feels like an understanding teacher or mentor. He can also be identified by flashes of purple that you sometimes might see in your peripheral vision when he is near. He communicates telepathically and is, therefore, excellent to call upon to communicate with all types of spirits that may not speak the same language as us. This also makes him the perfect archangel to help interpret dreams and signs.

Archangel Jophiel has a bright pink aura and a very feminine vibe. Her name means the *beauty of God*. She is one of the most uplifting, optimistic, and fun-loving of the archangels. She is relatively easy to identify because she will make you feel good about how you look. She will encourage you to take care of your physical surroundings, including decorating your home and wearing clothes that make you feel better about yourself. Anytime you need joy or beauty brought into your life, call on Archangel Jophiel.

Archangel Metatron, the Prophet Enoch, is also easy to identify. He is the scribe of the Akashic Records, which is where the records of everything past, present, and future are kept. He is known for his cube called Metatron's Cube, which contains all geometry shapes and can balance and clear chakras. He has a green and pink aura, but most importantly, he is highly motivated, energetic, and fiery. He is ready to get things moving. He does not mess around. However, he can also be quite philosophical. Call upon Metatron to connect with the vibration of most archangels.

Archangel Michael, the guardian of the south, fire, and summer, is one of the easiest archangels to identify; he is large and in charge. His name means *he who looks like God*, and he is the only angel to appear in the Bible, Quran, and Torah. He is massive, tall, and appears to humans as handsome. His aura is indigo or bright blue and purple with some gold. He carries a sword and shield of righteousness and light. One way to identify Michael is that he travels with legions of angels. The next time you call on Michael for protection consider that you probably have all the protection you need as long as you stay in his vibration. If Michael is protecting you, you're good. He can wield the right hand or left hand of God just as any spirit can show duality.

Another way to tell when Michael is around is the heat in a room or area will rise. It is a fiery, energetic heat that you will come to recognize as you work with Michael. Call on Michael for protection in any circumstance, no matter how small or insignificant it may seem or how large and overwhelming it may feel.

Archangel Raguel has a pale blue aura and a friendly, energetic attitude. His name means *friend of God*. When he is around, you will feel like you have a bodyguard that never has to get violent. There is just something about his energy that makes everyone around you behave in a civilized manner. He feels like a counselor that really cares about you. Raguel champions the underdog. Call upon him when you are fighting injustice.

Archangel Raphael, the guardian of the east, air, and spring, means *God heals*. He has a green aura and is a gentle, kind, and intelligent healer who often has green sparks of energy nearby. You can also recognize him by the caduceus he carries—a staff consisting of two entwined snakes. If you are any type of healer, call on Raphael for assistance. He is also helpful to those who travel or are in the business of travel, such as pilots or drivers.

Archangel Raziel is not as easily identified because he has a subtle, brilliant energy. His aura is rainbow translucence. His name means *secrets of God*, and he does not seem to reveal himself as quickly. Raziel will help you understand esoteric secrets and clear out any karma that does not serve you. He is much like Merlin in that he will help you with manifestation and your psychic abilities.

Archangel Sandalphon (Prophet Elijah) has a turquoise aura and is easily identified because of music. Whenever you sense a soft breeze with the soothing sounds of music in the distance, you are probably connecting with Sandalphon. If you are any type of artist or musician, call Sandalphon for assistance. Also, seek his assistance when attempting to communicate and connect with the various spirits of a different frequency than yours.

Archangel Uriel, the guardian of the north, Earth, and winter, means *God is light*. His aura is amber, and if you sense great wisdom combined with a candle or lantern, you can be certain Uriel is nearby. He may also hold a pentacle, the five-pointed star on a round disk representing the earth element. His wisdom and light are hard to ignore. Uriel will help you with everything from studying philosophy to understanding finances. He will also shed light on the truth of a matter when you are confused.

Archangel Zadkiel represents the *righteousness of God*. He has a rich, dark blue aura and extraordinarily calm and compassionate energy. Zadkiel is very needed on Earth at this time to help us have compassion for one another and find a path to forgiveness.

CONNECTING

The best way to connect with angels or archangels is to call on them and ask for their help. They typically will not interfere with your free will, so you need to call upon them for assistance. It is helpful to know how the various angels and archangels connect. It will be easier for you to feel confident in your connection.

For the most part, you can use the same methods covered in the first chapter (11 Steps to Broaden Your Frequency Bandwidth) to connect with angels and archangels. One powerful way to communicate with angels is through music. It can be any kind of music you'd like. It does not have to be what you think of as sacred or angelic music. They will reach you through songs. You may hear a song over and over again until the message finally gets through to you. Remember that the lyrics being used may be in a completely different context than the song's traditional meaning. (For example, love songs are very often used but without the romantic connotations.)

Crystals for Angels

There are some beautiful crystals for connecting with angels in general. You can wear these, meditate with them, put them beside your bed, or just carry them with you. Besides helping you connect with angels, these crystals will also help with other things in your life. For example, amethyst heightens spiritual awareness, helps intuition, and protects. Here are some others:

- Angelite increases psychic and spiritual awareness and aids astral travel.
- Apophyllite connects physical and spiritual realms and increases the energy of other crystals.
- Celestite aids in dream recall, especially related to angelic guidance.
- Selenite calms and focuses the mind while sharpening spiritual contact.

All archangels also have crystals that will help you connect with them specifically. One way to connect is through their aura color. If you can visualize an aura color, you can use that crystal color to connect to the archangel. Another way is to communicate through the properties of the crystal as they relate to the archangel.

Feathers

Many of you may have heard of feathers as being associated with angels and, as mentioned previously, theey may leave feathers for us as a sign. Likewise, spirit guides and loved ones may also utilize feathers as a way to send a signal. Read more about auras, chakras, crystals, and feathers in the appendix to this book.

Practice
Which Archangel Is Working with You Now?

The following will help you know which archangel you might already be connecting with at this time. The chakra system plays a very important role in adjusting your frequency. You can find more information regarding the chakra system in the appendix.

Place both feet on the ground, which sets an intention to connect to Mother Earth. Now, envision your crown chakra opening up and stretching up, up, up into the heavens. Take a slow, deep breath, and then just as slowly, let it out. Continue to inhale and exhale slowly and deeply for several more breaths. Finally, take one more deep breath and as you exhale, imagine that you are breathing out all the cares and worries from your day. Now is the time to call on any of your guides that you already know and ask them to assist you during this meditation. Ask Archangel Michael to join you from the angelic realm and travel with you on your journey.

As you continue to breathe, imagine roots growing up from the earth and covering your feet. Feel the beautiful warm energy from Mother Earth moving up through the soles of your feet and traveling up your legs while working its way to the root chakra, which is located in the area where you sit; its color is red.

Now envision the energy continuing up through your orange sacral chakra, which is about two finger widths below your navel. From there, the energy continues to move upward, going through your yellow solar plexus chakra, which is just below your ribs. Finally, the energy reaches your heart chakra in the middle of your chest and is a beautiful green. The energy from Mother Earth now mixes with the beautiful green energy of your heart chakra.

Now, shift your focus to the top of your head. Feel golden-white energy coming down from the heavens and entering through your violet crown chakra, which is at the top of your head. Next, this cosmic energy continues down through your indigo brow chakra, which is also called your third eye. From there, the energy flows down into your blue throat chakra. Finally, envision this Divine energy flowing down into your heart chakra, also mingling with its beautiful green energy.

Where these energies meet and mingle is also where you will meet your angels. As you continue to slowly breathe, try to focus on the pause between your inhale and your exhale. As you do this, visualize a path in front of you that leads into a dense forest. Begin to travel down this path. As you continue down the path, you become aware of a river running alongside it. Walk to the edge and enter the river. The water feels very soothing, and as you look down at the river's bottom, you see that it is covered with beautiful crystals in many different colors. Reach down and pick up a crystal. This is a gift for you from the angels. They want you to keep this crystal inside your heart. Place it there now.

It is time to continue your journey, and when you emerge from the water on the other side of the river, you continue walking down the path and through the forest. Soon, you become aware that you are coming to a beautiful hillside, and there on the trail you see Archangel Michael beckoning you to follow him. He leads you up the hillside to a structure. You notice a door into the structure, and Michael opens the door and shows you inside. You begin to take careful note of how the room looks, including all the colors you see.

You notice a table with chairs around it and go sit down at the table. Once you are comfortable, you look towards the door and see Archangel Michael ushering in an another archangel. This is the angel that you are to be working with at this time.

After your archangel enters, Michael closes the door. Michael is the protector, the bouncer at the door who will not let anyone or anything in that shouldn't be with you. You know you are safe. Now you turn your attention to the archangel Michael brought into the room. Carefully study the angel's appearance. You may only see a color or just sense a feeling. Slowly breathe and try to pick up on any of the angel's attributes that you can. Take another deep breath and take note of how you feel. What type of energy has the archangel brought into the room?

You look down at the table and notice there is a gift sitting on the table. The gift is from the archangel. Pick up the gift and open it. Take note of what is inside because you will receive a sign in the form of this gift within the next few days as confirmation in the physical world that you did indeed meet with an archangel. Now, you may ask your angel anything you wish, even if it is simply *What do I most need to know?* Or *How do I know when you are near me?*

When you have asked your questions, you notice Archangel Michael opening the door and beckoning you to join him. You rise from the table and say goodbye to the angel that has joined you, including Michael. You once again travel down the path, retracing your steps and leading you away from the structure, down the hillside, across the gentle river, and back through the forest to where you began your journey. Return your attention to your breath and back into your body. Stretch your arms and legs and shrug your shoulders. When you are ready, open your eyes.

Practice
11 Steps for Connecting with an Archangel

The following practice will give you steps to connect to a specific archangel to help with certain needs.

1. Start by calling on Metatron and Sandalphon to help get your frequency in line with the archangels or other angels. They both walked as humans and can recognize the human frequency and help adjust that frequency to the angel frequencies.

2. Decide what you want assistance, guidance, or help with in your life.

3. Based on the help you need, you can now pick one of the archangels mentioned in this chapter.

4. Once you know the archangel you want to work with, familiarize yourself with the attributes and signs associated with that archangel.

5. You want to familiarize yourself and set your intention of what you want before you call on an archangel so you know what to anticipate.

6. Based on the personality and characteristics of that archangel, you will now know what to watch for when you call upon the archangel.

7. Now you are ready to call on the archangel. It can be as simple as saying their name. Think of it this way, you may be traveling on an airplane and feel fearful. In that situation, there is no time to light a candle or do much of anything except call on a name. You know that Raphael is the archangel for travel, so you ask for his help. He will intervene just by invoking his name.

8. If you have the time, space, and circumstances, you may choose to do things to help you feel the presence of the archangel, such as lighting a candle that is the color associated with them or holding a crystal and saying the angel's name.

9. Still your mind and try to think of things associated with that archangel.

10. Close your eyes if possible or move around if that is more con-
    ducive to the connection you are trying to make.
11. Begin to sense the frequency change in not only your mind and
    body but also the environment and things around you.

PROTECTING

The archangels mentioned sound all love and light, don't they? Well, let
me be clear! Some of them, such as Archangel Michael and the legions
of angels that come with him when you call on him, are no joke. They
can, and they will, strike down anything that gets in the way of their
purpose.

There is an angel for everything on this Earth. Angels are messengers,
but they also have assignments. They have been represented as all love
and light, but maybe we should ask someone who has been on the receiving end of Michael's sword of flame how loving it felt!

Does this mean you need to protect yourself from Archangel
Michael? To answer that, you might want to ask yourself if you believe
you are on the side of righteousness, which he represents. Keep in mind
that different religions throughout the ages have been convinced that
their side was the one of righteousness. At the same time, their enemy
thought the same thing.

While Archangel Michael is typically thought of as one of the *good
guys*, it all just depends on your point of view (whether or not you are on
the receiving end of his sword). This is true of all angels at every level,
and we should not be quick to judge whether their actions are good
or bad, positive or negative, of the light or the dark. In general, with a
few potential exceptions such as fallen angels, it is safe to assume that
ultimately angels are here to serve the highest good of humanity overall.
Sometimes, their actions may not seem so in the moment, but when all
is said and done, the *why* may become apparent to us.

When deciding which angels we want to work with, it becomes vital
to consider each angel's primary *vibration* (they can vary their frequency
at will). The speed at which energy particles are moving determines their
frequency and, depending on our own frequency, being exposed to different frequencies can affect us in many ways. Some frequencies may
feel soothing, comforting, or even energizing. They may elicit feelings of

safety, happiness, or inspiration. While not necessarily unpleasant, other frequencies may take some getting used to before we are completely comfortable around them. And finally, we may find some frequencies that make us uncomfortable and prefer not to be around. For this reason, we must discover whether a particular angel's vibration is compatible with our own. We will either vibe with it, or we won't, and we need to find out.

How do we do that? We try it. Just like you would with the other spirit guides in chapter 1, you can do the same thing with angels and archangels. Does this angel or archangel seem to fit your vibe or vibration? If not, perhaps you should consider working with an angel that can help you change your vibration. If you feel lost in life, overwhelmed, and tired, adjusting your own frequency may be an excellent place to start working with angels and archangels.

Ask yourself if your current vibration is serving you well. There is no implied judgment in that question. Still, it's an important consideration to make. It will play into your decision of whether or not to work with a particular guide or angel. Pay attention to how a specific angel or archangel makes you feel, and you will begin to notice changes in your own vibration. Suppose you choose to work with angels in particular frequencies. In that case, you may need protection, and there also may be some angels that are at a vibration you don't care to even encounter.

Typically, you do not need to protect against archangels because you have to call upon them to help you in the first place. However, there could be situations where you need protection from any potential fallout resulting from working with a particular archangel. For instance, if someone has stolen something from you and you call upon Archangel Chamuel to help you find it, you may want to ask for protection regarding the potential repercussions of ratting someone out (e.g., retaliation, denial, attack, etc.). Another example where you might ask for protection is when you call upon an archangel on behalf of someone suffering. Again, it is an excellent idea to protect yourself in this situation so as not to take on that energy of suffering yourself.

Suppose you decide you need protection due to working with a particular angel for a specific purpose. In that case, the best way to go about it is to enlist help from another angel. Start by calling on the archangel that you want to work with for a particular purpose. Next, call upon the angel from which you wish to request backup. (You can see why you must learn how to distinguish between the different frequencies of angels). Ask this second angel to work on your behalf to offset any potential repercussions from working with the first archangel.

Whenever you are hesitant or feel concerned about the possible consequences of working with archangels, it is always a good idea to call for backup. This ensures you are protected and that the situation will work out for your highest good. Note that Archangel Michael is probably the best angel to call upon to protect you from any potential physical danger but working with Michael can be tricky because of his intensity. If you find yourself in a difficult situation due to working with Michael, I advise seeking the counsel of Uriel for wisdom and then Raziel to adjust all the frequencies within the situation, including your own.

COLLABORATING

Angels and archangels want to collaborate with us. They honor our free will and will not push themselves on us, but the minute we ask for help, they are there! We can identify and connect with them easily once we know what to look for and can identify their individual frequencies. Whether it is our guardian angel that is always with us or a special angel we call in to help with a specific task, they are available to help and guide us the moment we ask (which is why they certainly can fall under the category of spirit guide). They are just an angelic form of spirit guide.

When you want to call on specific characteristics of Source, such as forgiveness, you will know that an archangel exists for that very characteristic, and you only need to solicit the help of that particular archangel. In the case of forgiveness, Archangel Zadkiel would be ideal. Of course, there are more angels than the ones we will talk about here, but this will give you a good idea of how an archangel might be able to help you. You will know how to identify them, and then you need to know how to collaborate with them.

Deciding Which Archangel You Need on Your Team

The following will help you know which archangel to call upon when you need someone to guide you or to collaborate with you.

- Archangel Ariel will help when you want to help an animal or the environment. She also will help with any of your physical needs. That is broad, so you might want to get to know Archangel Ariel.

- Archangel Azrael will not only help you when it is your time to transition but perhaps more importantly, any time you grieve. He helps ministers, hospice workers, first responders, and those who have lost a loved one. He is ready and waiting to help with any kind of grief you are experiencing.

- Archangel Chamuel is excellent to collaborate with to find anything you have lost, no matter how big or small. From losing your purpose in life to losing your keys, you can call out to Chamuel for help.

- Archangel Gabriel is perfect to work with when trying to give birth to anything from an idea to adopting a child/animal companion to issues with fertility.

- Archangel Haniel is the perfect archangel to have on your team when you are dealing with any feminine issue. Haniel will also help you with clairvoyance (clear seeing with your mind's eye).

- Archangel Jeremiel is ready when you need help with significant life changes and the emotions that go along with those. He also will step in and help you forgive yourself and others.

- Archangel Jophiel helps you see the positivity and beauty where you can't seem to find it. This includes things such as decorating your house or picking out clothes to uplift your spirits.

- Archangel Metatron is there for you when you are working with gifted children that others are trying to tell you need medication to calm them down. These children are always gifted children. Of course, go to the doctors and specialists of your choice, but keep Metatron in the loop.

- Archangel Raguel will help you resolve disputes. He will serve as the mediator.

- Archangel Raphael is ready to jump in to help anytime there is a matter involving a need for healing.

- Archangel Raziel will help you manifest and bring magic into your life.

- Archangel Sandalphon will collaborate with singers and musicians. Make him a member of your band. Also let him help you connect with other frequencies.
- Archangel Uriel will give you wisdom when you seem at a loss to discern the truth.
- Archangel Zadkiel will collaborate with you on anything from studying and memorization to helping with forgiveness.

HONORING

Angels and archangels do not expect to be worshipped, nor do they want to be. However, as with anyone, they do like to be acknowledged and appreciated, so you might want to show your gratitude for their help. This can be as simple as saying *thank you for your help*, but you may also choose to show them honor in other ways. For example, if you wear jewelry with their name or image, you are honoring them. You can light candles in their tribute or carry a crystal that you associate with them. Many things you would do to honor them are the same things you would do to connect with them. The use of their color, crystals, or symbols enhances your connection with them while simultaneously honoring them.

DEMYSTIFYING

While most humans believe in angels, the beliefs typically come from their culture or religious upbringing. But we do know that there seems to be a fairly universal agreement that they exist. However, there are a lot of misconceptions. Some angels are mighty and fierce. When someone says they are calling on Archangel Michael for protection, they need to realize they are calling in a powerful warrior. While guardian angels may be loving and caring most of the time in the ways they exhibit their love and protection, archangels may be called upon for some of the tough stuff we don't like to think about.

The sad fact is that there have been religious wars throughout history. Everything from spiritual texts to archeological findings points to the belief that archangels do indeed have duality, just like every energy. One country might see the archangel as the hero while the other considers the archangel as the tyrant. The judgment of energy is a matter of perspective, and there is no distinction without comparison.

Many will differentiate between angels and people in the sense that angels never were human. However, we know there are exceptions to this in Metatron and Sandalphon. I invite you to consider that there are many more exceptions than these two. There are angels among us in human form. How small-minded of us to think otherwise.

Even though angels are depicted with wings, that is not typically how I have seen them (although, my perception of them has undoubtedly evolved, or perhaps they have). As energy beings, they are more than capable of changing their form. I also have seen them look much more extraterrestrial than as human with wings.

Ultimately, anything and everyone could change form if the power of transmutation—the ability to change energetic form—was truly utilized. There are lots of hierarchal archetypes surrounding archangels. While these may or may not be accurate, it is more important to realize that they can and will work with you. Once you do, you will know how they show up for you.

4
Loved Ones in Spirit (Ancestors)

At one time, I was working for a psychic fair where I would do twenty-four sessions of fifteen-minutes each, and I was almost always sold out. Towards the end of one particular Sunday, a beautiful young woman named Ashlie walked up to my table, sat down, and quietly asked what I could tell her for the day. She seemed exhausted physically yet had an other-worldly aspect to her.

The minute she sat down, I sensed a young man around her. I asked him to show me who he was, and I quickly realized it was her brother. Images began flooding into my mind's eye. I asked Ashlie if her brother had recently died by suicide, and she confirmed he had—the day before this fair. I expressed it did not feel entirely ethical to do a reading the day after his passing, but she implied she had already had other poor intuitive readings that day. I hesitantly agreed to carry on with a quick message of hope.

I knew right away that for this young woman hope was in the form of an answer to how he had died. I am a compassionate reader, but I am always honest. I told her that what she and her family had been told about his passing was not an accurate account. Still, without any information from Ashlie, I told her that her brother had hanged himself in a backyard on some sort of wooden beam or maybe a clothesline. I knew this was an essential point because her brother kept emphasizing it. I also gave Ashlie a brief description of how her brother had looked in the fullness of life. I grinned a little and added that he was pretty sure of himself. She quietly laughed and said that was true.

However, at that point, Ashlie told me thank you, and she appreciated my kindness but the way I described the suicide was not what had occurred. That was interesting to me because her brother was still there with Ashlie and seemed to care that the facts were resolved. Of course,

I gave her my deepest sympathies and offered her my card should she want to reach out to me.

Some weeks later, Ashlie did reach out. She still spoke in a soft and subdued voice. She told me that she thought I had been correct when I gave her the reading, but that was not what she had been told or what other people there had told her about the incident. Ashlie knew it was best that her mother not read the police report, so Ashlie read it. Upon receiving the complete police report, she learned I had correctly described how her brother had passed, which answered some additional questions surrounding his death. Some police reports are skim as to details, but this one was comprehensive.

Ashlie was, like many, concerned about what dying by suicide would mean for her brother's eternal soul. I assured her I saw him whole at this point, meaning that he had crossed to the light. He was not in any kind of purgatory or hell. In fact, I have never seen that, even though I was raised to believe it.

It is essential to point out that the term "committed suicide" implies a stigma. We would never say "committed cancer" or "committed a heart attack." Those who die of suicide should have no judgment or stigma placed on them, because I assure you there is no judgment placed on them in the afterlife and in higher self-beingness.

I went on to tell Ashlie he was still a bit full of himself. She laughed once again. As it turns out, Ashlie is quite possibly one of the most psychic people I know. We understand each other on a level that neither of us can relate to many, even in this business. Her brother brought us together, and of course, he is very full of himself about that.

Most importantly, the reading she received gave her closure. She was also validated in knowing she was not alone in believing that the original story about her brother was not valid. It only took a few words, genuinely from her brother, for her to know that there was more to the story. The police report then validated her knowingness and gave her closure and peace.

Unlike what many mediums tell you—that they primarily get messages from a departed loved one to convey how much they love those still on Earth—that is usually not my experience. I tend to ask for and receive specifics to let the grieving one know that I genuinely am in touch with their loved one. There is usually something they need for closure. The specifics help the one who is grieving trust the message. Then I always let them know they can get in touch with their loved ones without my help, but I'm always there if they need me. Of course, the departed one will typically convey their love, but they usually have other things they want to say. The ones that really speak about love are the ones that did not convey it as much when they were in human form.

THE FLIP SIDE

There are loved ones we do not want anything to do with even after they die. Just because they have left their human form does not mean they are angels. Some are the same jerks or perverts they were when they were in human form. Death does not automatically make you whole or absolved.

I mentioned my self-destructive phase earlier in the book. Part of that phase involved someone I would certainly never want to hear from again. The person did significant damage to my life.

At one point, I was receiving a reading from one of the SoulTopian mediums named Nellie. It was a quick fifteen-minute reading during one of our discounted days we call SoulTopia Sensation. I honestly just sat down because she had an opening, which was unusual.

Nellie opened the session with these words, "Someone says, *I will find you when you least expect it.*" There are quite possibly no more frightening words that anyone could speak to me. I knew exactly who was saying that to me, and I knew the person was deceased. I was foolish enough to think I was finally free of the person. I looked at Nellie and told her I did not want to hear anything more from that spirit.

Poor Nellie is one of the nicest people I know. You see, I had never told anyone except my doctors about the threat the person had always made to me that struck fear in me like nothing else can strike fear in me. I never want to hear another message from that spirit, yet I know the spirit kept its word and *found me when I least expected it.*

Ashlie also has had an encounter with a spirit with whom she does not want to communicate. Ashlie was raised by an aunt who *severely* abused her. Because Ashlie was so brilliant, her school finally caught on when her behavior was changing. Fortunately, Ashlie was removed from her aunt's home. Unfortunately, the aunt never apologized for the horrific abuse. Through the years, the aunt began to suffer numerous chronic health issues, which became her hell. When the aunt finally died a very tragic death, Ashlie did not care or attend the funeral.

Since her passing, the aunt has tried to talk to Ashlie several times. The aunt will walk up behind Ashlie on the left side. Ashlie wants no part of this conversation and says, *NO! I will not talk with you.* Ashlie clarifies that she realizes she is still connected to this aunt, and she has forgiven her. However, she chose never to be part of the woman's life once she was free from her aunt while she was alive, and it is no different now that she is in a spirit form. Ashlie has chosen not to engage in that energy. Just because Ashlie's aunt has died does not mean she has changed her ways.

INTRODUCING

Perhaps some of the most important energetic spirits are our loved ones. Unfortunately, in the West, we speak much of birth but very little of death. Hopefully, this fear of death will change if we truly embrace the reality of life after death and the ability to communicate with our loved ones. Once we can accept, or at the very least consider, the concept that there is no veil, more of us may begin to realize how easy it is to communicate with all spirits.

I see the so-called other side. I have never understood when people talk of a veil or a mystical barrier between worlds, realms, dimensions, or planes. Perhaps the veil is a construct of humans to keep us from realizing we can contact our loved ones and other energetic beings. Please know your loved ones are with you. Yes, they have passed on to another vibrational state of beingness, but they are also with you. Even for those who do not sense or see their loved ones, I assure you they are there.

You cannot see radio waves, but you know they exist. Our loved ones in spirit are now vibrating at a different frequency. Some find it easier to tap into that radio channel than others, but your loved one is whole and vibrating at a high rate of love and compassion.

IDENTIFYING

This mythical veil is the most significant barrier to sensing or identifying your loved one who has passed. Fear can build walls of many kinds. The construct of a veil is simply a wall between what is really only varying vibrations of energy. This age-old myth that has been perpetuated keeps people from realizing just how close their loved ones are to them. To sense your loved ones, start to believe they are with you or at least be open to the possibility of them being with you. In other words, open your mind to the possibility, if only just a little bit.

This is not to give you false hope. This is to let you know the truth. Those who have passed are still living but in a different energetic state. Even if you are skeptical, I am going to ask you to consider some things. Have you ever thought your loved one was near, but you dismissed it as your imagination? Have you ever heard them whisper your name and thought you were just tired? Have you had them come to you in your dreams and thought, *what a pleasant dream*? Have you ever felt they were trying to get your attention through signs like a bird outside your window, but you dismissed the idea?

Why not open up to the idea instead? While not every single bird you see may be a message from your loved one, don't miss the message by dismissing it as wishful thinking. Your loved ones can communicate with you in numerous ways, and they will if you will let them.

One of the main things to remember about our loved ones who have passed is that they still have their personalities intact. Just because they are not here anymore does not mean they are perfect angels. If they used to nag you about cleaning your room, they will still nag you about cleaning your room. If they always wanted you to get married to that sweet kid down the street, they may still bring up the fact that you missed out by not marrying the perfect one who got away. In other words, they will tell you what they think, and if they have an agenda, it does not magically disappear.

They may eventually begin to see things from a higher perspective, but do not think their personality will completely disappear. This is a great way to identify them. They will also talk to you or try to communicate with you in a way you will recognize. It could be an interest you shared, or something they really enjoyed that you associate with them. Keep in mind that should you see them with your physical vision or in your mind's eye, they will usually appear as they were at the most memorable time in their life. Usually, this correlates to the happiest time in their life. Still, please know that sometimes they will appear as they were during an unfortunate time or even during their last moments before death. This is not meant to hurt you. This is their way of letting you know it really is them or perhaps giving you closure or clarity.

Practice
11 Ways to Know Your Loved One Is with You

The following will help you know when a loved one in spirit is around you. Use this list to practice becoming aware of the loved ones around you. You will also begin to differentiate the energy of loved ones from other energetic beings.

1. Aromas—Smell is your most robust sense connected to memory. First, think of your loved one and their favorite scent. Now think of the smell that most reminds you of them. Both are important because your loved one may send the smell of what they remember, such as the scent of leather in their favorite car, or they may send you a scent of what you remember, such as the cologne they wore.

2. Dreams—This typically will be a dream that wakes you up or lingers with you when you wake up. It's as if you cannot shake the dream.

3. Photos—The spirits of loved ones will often communicate through photos. We once had an employee at SoulTopia who painted. She had painted one picture for her grandfather, and it hung on the wall behind the checkout area. This painting often was askew on the wall, but on more than one occasion, we have observed it fly off the wall when she was speaking of her grandfather.

   Another way spirits will communicate through photos is on your phone. You will find a photo begin to pop up out of order. I have one image of a client who passed away that pops up all the time on my phone. I have thousands of photos, but this one photo pops up frequently. This is a client I had encouraged to see a doctor because I detected he had cancer in his throat even though there were no visible signs of cancer.

   He first came to me as a strong man who rode a motorcycle. When I met him, the first thing I said was that I was not a doctor, but he needed to see one because I was sure he had never visited his doctor. He laughed and left the appointment. About a year later, he came into my store to tell me he was dying of throat cancer, and he should have listened to me. It broke my heart. It was an occasion when I had really hoped I was wrong, but it turned out that I wasn't. I have kept the photo of him on his motorcycle in my phone because he was so proud of that photo. He pops up every now and again to remind me that my ability to sense cancer is one I should not shy away from or try to explain or defend, but instead use for good.

4. Electricity—Spirits can easily manipulate electricity. As an aside, the more you work with your psychic abilities, the more you will affect electricity. Loved ones will communicate in all kinds of ways through electricity, even electric toothbrushes.

5. Windchimes—Even though windchimes are often outside nowadays, they used to be placed inside homes and buildings to detect the movement of spirits. So, your loved ones will communicate to you through chimes and may even make a particular song for you.

6. Feathers—Feathers are covered in detail in chapter 2 and the appendix, but not only do angels and archangels communicate with feathers but loved ones do as well. Refer to the appendix for the significance of some of the colors.

7. Shapes—Loved ones may leave you signs of love through everyday objects in the shape of hearts. This depends on how romantic the loved one was while in human form. If they would have considered that silly, they would not suddenly start doing it once they were in spirit form.

8. Symbols—Look for symbols in your everyday life that seem like something your loved one would leave you. For example, if they loved to read and suddenly a book's pages are fluttering in the wind on a chair, don't dismiss it as happenstance. Instead, look for communication everywhere, and you will find it.

9. Numbers—Spirits of all kinds use numbers and repetition to communicate. If your loved one had a favorite number, you might notice that number appearing in different ways. They may also send messages with numbers related to you or the two of you as a couple.

10. Birds—Birds are beautiful messengers from spirits. Loved ones will most certainly communicate through these winged creatures. Doves, bluebirds, and cardinals are some of the birds most associated with communication from loved ones.

11. Songs—All spirits seem to communicate through song, but none more so than loved ones. So, although these messages may make you sad at first, inevitably, they come to be welcome blessings from your loved ones.

CONNECTING

You will find that the many ways of identifying a loved one, as shown in the previous practice, will be similar to and entwine with how you connect with them. As with any energy being, the best way to communicate with them is to believe you can. Just be open to the possibility that you are not imagining the connection. One of the first ways they may come to you is to whisper your name. So, it is important not to dismiss things you might hear. Listen for them. Of course, a balance is needed with all of this in that you want to continue to live your life because your loved one would like you to do so. In fact, often, if you are unable to connect with your loved one, they do not want you to become dependent on that connection and not go on with your life.

One of the most common ways our loved ones begin reaching out to us is through signs. The signs they may use are infinite in number. Still, as with other energy beings, repetition of a number or hearing a song, or seeing their favorite animal are a few of the common ones. If you used to play cards together, get out your cards and start a game. If you used to dance together, turn on the music and begin to dance. Go to the places you used to go and do the things you used to do. The same goes for the things they used to enjoy. Even if you did not play golf, but they loved to golf, get out the clubs, or go play a round. Play their favorite music. Eat their favorite foods. Wear their favorite scent.

This may seem difficult at first, so do these things as you feel ready. Keep in mind that our loved ones are not in some land far away. I encourage you to remember this and to talk to them, acknowledge their presence. This will go a long way towards dispelling your doubt and helping you recognize signs that they are still with you.

One purpose of this book is to let you know spirits, including your departed loved ones, really do move among us much more than you think. Can they materialize into a solid form? Although it may not be common, it can happen. Everything is energy. It merely changes forms. If the energy changed once, why can't it change again? However, most of the time that is not how it happens, and instead we sense our loved ones with our inner knowing.

If you feel you cannot perceive or connect with your loved one—while this can be very upsetting—there are numerous reasons. You may not be emotionally ready to connect, or they just may be busy at the moment. (Yes, they have lives too.) When you feel like they are not connecting with you, it may be the very time they are doing the most work on your behalf. However, if you get really discouraged, you can always seek out a suitable medium.

There are some tools that will help you get into a state of mind where you can more easily connect with your loved ones. Meditation, crystals, candles, aromatherapy, music, and altars of remembrance may help you begin to connect. Crystals to help you connect with deceased loved ones are lapis lazuli and record keeper quartz crystals. Essential oils are also beneficial. For example, the blue lotus, revered in ancient Egypt, is ideal for connecting with departed loved ones. Florida Water, a well-known spiritual cleansing water, is also helpful because it helps clear the *static,* so to speak, allowing you to more easily connect to other frequencies. Finally, burning herbs or incense such as marigold can help you connect with passed loved ones because herbs are also known to shift the vibrational frequency of energy.

Practice
11 Steps to Match Frequencies in the Future

The following is intended for loved ones to perform together while still in their earthly forms. It is a plan of sorts of how to meet when one or the other passes to spiritual form so that they will more easily be able to match frequencies.

1. Make a plan with a loved one before one of you leaves the human form. It helps for both of you to write it down. The more you are connected in this frequency, the more you will easily connect when one of you is in spirit form.

2. Decide how often it will be healthy for you to lean on the other one in spirit. Again, talk about this while you are both in human form.

3. Decide on a place where you would meet.

4. Decide on a catchphrase that you will know is a message from your loved one.

5. Decide on an aroma that is a message from your loved one.

6. Decide on a song that is a message from your loved one.

7. Decide on sequences of numbers that are a message from your loved one.

8. Decide on a symbol that is a message from your loved one.

9. Decide on an animal that is a message from your loved one.

10. Decide which type of electrical equipment the loved one will communicate through after the loved one has passed.

11. Clarify when a sign is a warning versus a reminder of love.

PROTECTING

The most considerable protection you may need to put in place is from anyone who mistreated you when they were alive and with whom you do not want to connect after they have passed. That drunk uncle is likely still a jerk, and you may not want anything more to do with him when he is dead than you did when he was living. That is just fine. You are in charge. Do not invite him to the party, and if he tries to come anyway, simply kick him out of your mind and bar the door!

You also may need more time to grieve and heal than you realize. It is dangerous for you to become addicted to living in the past. Your loved one would not want that for you, and that could easily be the reason you do not receive signs or messages from them right away. If, for that reason, you choose to seek out a medium, be sure to get a referral.

Keep in mind that even if someone does give you a referral, you may not click with the same person that your best friend does. The medium could be genuinely gifted and legitimate. Still, if their energy does not jive with yours, it may be better to keep looking. Also, before you get discouraged by the results of a reading, try to get solid evidence that the medium is actually talking to your loved one. (When doing this, be careful not to become the victim of a cold reading! Cold readings involve high-probability guesses based on the medium picking up on cues from you, your reactions to what they are saying, and even your body language.)

Not everyone who claims to be a medium truly is one. Even if they are sometimes successful, they often are not consistently so. I advise avoid going to anyone of which you are unsure if you are grieving. If they cannot connect with your loved one, it could easily do more harm than good.

Personally speaking, unless my client has known me and my work a long time, I always get the loved one to give me something specific so the client can know I am genuinely talking to their loved one. Sometimes a reading can get crowded with a lot of other spirits showing up and wanting to speak. For that reason, ask the medium to ask the spirit for something specific so you will feel confident they are talking to your loved one.

COLLABORATING

Unlike other energy beings that usually do not interfere with our free will, our loved ones may get right in the middle of our affairs. They will help and guide us, but remember they will have their personalities. Do not be surprised if they have strong opinions even after death. Remember, even though they are no longer in a physical body, as far as they are concerned, they are very much still alive, perhaps even more so. Their spirit is indeed evolving, but energy beings evolve over time and at different paces, and it doesn't mean they suddenly become fully enlightened when they are no longer in physical form.

Hopefully, our loved ones will gain some insight after death that will allow them to conspire on our behalf to some extent. They will typically try to help us in similar ways they would have when they were in a human form. If they were manipulative in life, they would probably be manipulative in spirit. If, while alive, they only gave you suggestions for ways to address a problem, you may now receive little spirit nudges. I have heard many mothers and grandmothers comment on the way their daughters are wearing their hair. Sometimes it is complementary and sometimes it is not. The point is that the loved one still has their ego-mind, and most are not hesitant to express it.

HONORING

If you enjoyed the loved one, honor them in the way they wanted to be celebrated in life. Remember, there is no veil. They are with you now. They are just in another form with a different vibration. If you adhere to a belief that worships ancestors, such as Yoruba, Santeria, or Shinto, then certainly adhere to whatever form of honoring that ancestor is right for you. Many cultures will set up altars for deceased loved ones. Some will keep a candle burning to represent the safe travel of the immortal soul. If this is your religious or cultural belief, then, by all means, carry on with those beliefs and traditions. Otherwise, just talk with the loved one and commune with them just as you did when they lived. This does not make you crazy. On the contrary, it will help you connect with your loved one.

DEMYSTIFYING

Many of us have accepted most of the things we have been taught about death and dying, heaven, hell, and purgatory without ever attempting on our own to *sense* the accuracy of these teachings. Try to let go of your existing bias and consider that perhaps all those teachings could be wrong based on belief systems that have been passed down for generations and unconditionally accepted despite evidentiary proof to the contrary.

The opinions I am sharing with you based on my own experiential observations are beginning to be supported by discoveries made in physics (e.g., the properties of energy, planes, dimensions, realms). The most important thing I want to share with you regarding the death of loved ones is that they are still close to you. You are separated only by a vibrational difference in your frequencies. My hope is that you will learn to sense their vibration to communicate with them.

Another thing I would like to assure you is that if someone you loved left the physical plane via taking their own life, they are in precisely the same place that the people who died from natural causes are (and *that place* is very close and accessible to you). There is no punishment for someone who emotionally suffered in life to the extent of taking their own life. The only *punishment* they experience may be self-inflicted due to regret they feel for the pain they caused their loved ones.

Another misconception is that someone is crazy if they think they can communicate with loved ones who have passed. The whole premise of this book disputes that. Someone may also tell you that it is unhealthy to try to communicate with departed loved ones, and to them I would say *not necessarily so*. As long as there is balance, like with everything else, it can actually be a source of comfort to those grieving and speed the process of healing. I concede that it is important to continue to live your life and not allow yourself to become obsessed with holding onto the past, but that does not preclude acknowledging that your loved one is still around you and taking comfort in that fact. Do not let anyone tell you it is *time to move on* and leave the past in the past. There is no reason you cannot *move on* and still be aware that your loved one is with you!

If you are wondering about paranormal events associated with disincarnate spirits, of course this phenomenon exists. There are many types of spirits that are resistant to leave the physical plane. I just don't see them as paranormal or out of the ordinary. The idea of spirits walking among us on Earth is very typical.

As discussed previously, personalities tend to remain the same whether they are in physical form or in spirit. It is possible that someone miserable in life has difficulty freeing themselves from their suffering. When they die, their unhappiness keeps them tethered to the physical plane. People who experienced a very traumatic death often were not ready to leave, and so they either have not accepted that they are no longer alive in the physical world, or they simply try to stay.

Other spirits resist leaving this plane due to an abnormally strong emotional attachment to a person or place. Some spirits simply are very fearful of death, believing they will be punished for the life they led while they were here. Some spirits merely get great satisfaction from hurting others, and they stick around because it allows them to continue to do so.

And finally, an oft-repeated myth that happens to be one of my major pet peeves: Some claim that mediums are the only ones who can communicate with anyone who has died. They usually go on to say *all mediums are psychics, but not all psychics are mediums*. Let me be clear about how false that is. Anyone can communicate with spirits, whether they identify as a medium, a psychic, or neither. It's simply a matter of developing your ability to sense the subtleties of frequency. I can do it, and YOU can do it, and don't let anyone tell you that you can't!

As a matter of fact, it has been my experience as a medium that people sometimes come to me for one type of reading only to have a loved one or missing person come through in the reading. This has happened notably in two high-profile situations. I have permission to relay one of the stories to you, but I will not use the name of the girl involved because I do not want to exploit her murder in any way. My point in relaying this story to you is to emphasize how much I disagree with those mediums who are egotistical regarding their alleged ability to communicate with those who have passed. Please hear me. They, just like me, know how to tune into that frequency for some reason. I also believe the spirit finds them.

Allow me to explain through the story of this reading for Tanya, who has helped me recall most of the details as I usually forget my readings. When I contacted Tanya, she said she vividly remembered the reading. This is a summary of the events surrounding that reading.

Tanya made an appointment for a mediumship reading with me after receiving a strong recommendation from a friend that she do so. I never take appointments in my home, but I was prompted to do just that for the session with Tanya, although we had never met. When she arrived, she informed me that she wanted to see who would come through in the reading. She specifically was hoping to hear from her brother and best friend.

Tanya tells me that I asked her not to give me any details, and then I proceeded to describe specifics about them and exactly how they had died. I also received information from her mother. However, a petite blonde young woman around the age of 18-24 suddenly was so strongly in my head, and she was loud. She was not loud in an angry or screaming way, but in a way a student in class would want to be called on by the teacher. I relayed all of this to Tanya, and her mouth dropped open.

Meanwhile, the young woman kept talking to me, and then I got a piercing headache. Tanya recalls that I grabbed my head and told Tanya that I was sorry. I was battling my severe head pain with my need to remain professional. I managed to say *something has happened to this young woman*. At that point, Tanya interjected. She was having a little trouble gaining her composure because apparently, I was saying some things unknown to the public. As it turns out, the young woman was missing and the subject of an investigation into what was beginning to look like murder. Tanya was a close friend of the family and remains so to this day. Tanya told me she was part of the search party looking for the young woman and that they sadly needed to find her body if she had fallen prey to a killer.

This part of the story I do remember very well. I remember telling Tanya that the young woman did not want to be found, but they would ultimately find her farther north than where they were searching. Here is one of the most important reasons I am conveying this story: The young woman did not want to be found because she liked the fact that it was bringing her family closer together. She was not talking about the trial to me. She was talking about her family and the fact that it was healing old wounds during the most unimaginable tragedy. The young woman had a much different perspective.

Another reason I tell this story is because yes, I was extremely accurate on many details I had no way of knowing. That is not new to me. Some will call it spot on. But you see, that is not the point. It does not make me gifted or special. In fact, the young woman was coming through Tanya. Apparently, details came out that Tanya learned later, so I wasn't just reading Tanya's thoughts (which is what many mediums do versus actually connecting with the spirit of the one who has passed). The young woman knew Tanya could be trusted. She knew Tanya loved her and cared for her. The one who had the gift was Tanya. I was a mere messenger. When you learn to expand your broadband frequency, you will be able to connect with any spirit you want.

Tanya did ask me that day to talk to the family because many other psychic mediums had tried to garner attention by contacting the family with inaccurate information or vague information, such as "she wants you to know she loves you."

Let's address that. I have read many books where mediums tell you this is the main thing spirits will relay to them. Well…okay. It really doesn't take a psychic medium to tell someone that their loved one in spirit loves them yet provides no details. Personally, I question the veracity of a reading with no details because that has never been my experience. Passed loved ones give details, and they typically have an agenda of some sort. Perhaps it is because when I give a reading I get something from the spirit that lets the person confirm that I am indeed talking to their loved one. I need some proof, and I want to give it to my clients. If they're going to say I love you, that is great, but they will need to let me know something to definitively identify themselves first.

But back to me talking to her parents—frankly, it scared me. I am a lawyer, and I knew that getting involved might open me up to criticism. How selfish of me—I know. But in my defense, I didn't want to mess anything up in the case, and I also didn't want to be *that* psychic.

After talking to Tanya recently, I am pretty certain she did let the family know. And yes! The young woman's murderer was brought to justice, and her body was found later. As I had described, it was north of where they had been looking.

5

Animal Spirits

Sarah is a single woman I met about ten years ago. Her cats are her children, and I often call her the mother of cats. Sarah had a cat named Mystic with whom she was extremely close. After Mystic *crossed the rainbow bridge*, we knew that Mystic was hanging around in spirit, watching over Sarah. Mystic also watched over her other cat, which he most certainly bossed around but was quite fond of while in physical form.

About two years after Mystic's passing, Sarah moved to a high-rise condominium. One night Sarah was sleeping when she felt a cat paw hit her. It was not a slight tap of the paw; it was more like a slap. Sarah sat up to see which of her then three cats was hitting her. It was none of them. It was then that she sensed the presence of her Himalayan cat Mystic, and Mystic was wanting her to get up and get moving.

A little tired but now awake, Sarah began to smell smoke. Mystic was emphatic now. Mystic wanted her to get the other cats and get out! Sarah grabbed the other cats as fast as she could and ran out of her condo and the high-rise, only to watch the entire condominium burn down moments later. Her Mystic had saved her life and the life of the other three cats.

Sarah is quick to note that sometimes animals also come to us for help. At one point, she was sitting in her all-white living room and very clearly saw a white cat. Sarah thought it was her Himalayan Mystic in spirit but then realized this was a different spirit. Sarah was very accustomed to seeing animals in spirit, so this did not surprise her. The difference was that it was usually a cat she knew or was familiar with from the past. Nothing else eventful occurred that evening, and Sarah had a restful night's sleep.

The following day as she was driving to work, she took her regular route. She saw a white cat injured on the side of the road. Of course, she was devastated. She immediately thought of the white spirit cat in her living room. This cat was the same spirit cat. He had appeared to her the night before, and she sprang into action and sat with him while he crossed the rainbow bridge. He still visits her from time to time.

Animals need us, and we need them. We rely on each other's energy to help lift our spirits. Animals may be actual pets in our lives, or they may be guides in our lives. No matter how animals interact with us, we are so incredibly fortunate to have our energetic forms interact in magnificent ways.

THE FLIP SIDE

If all energy has duality, does this mean that animals in spirit can exhibit a lower frequency? In other words, can an animal in spirit choose to be evil? I propose to you yes, just as all energy can. I immediately think of hell hounds—the dogs said to guard and assist demons. Japanese folklore has a perfect example of an animal that exhibits duality. Kitsune, the Japanese word for fox, gain a more extraordinary paranormal ability the older they become. This fox can shape-shift into human form. Some use their powers to trick humans, while some use them to help humans. The point is that they have duality and can choose the whole range on the duality spectrum, but they can also choose where they want to vibe.

INTRODUCING

Animals are energy beings, just like anything else is an energy being. At some point, we adopted the erroneous idea that humans are the center of all. This mistaken assumption is sadly apparent now on Earth as we see what has occurred with our ecosystem. We are no more superior than any other type of being. We all play a role, and that is the cycle of evolution instead of the hierarchy of evolution that so many want to adopt and hold dear.

With that in mind, we know humans can do things that animals cannot do in physical form and vice versa. Many cultures have revered certain animals and understand this much better than other cultures. For our purposes, we will use the term animal spirits broadly to encapsulate all those beings of the earth, water, sky, etc. Indigenous cultures have long used the term spirit animal, particularly in Shamanic practices. These spirit animals are traditionally believed to choose you. They may guide you, but their purpose is typically for a particular lesson. There are also animal totems of the indigenous peoples. The clan traditionally calls upon or invokes the animal totem on behalf of the entire group, not an individual.[9]

There are also power animals. Power animals have similar traits to the individual and unite with them. An animal guide might upgrade to a power animal in some cases. Finally, there is a familiar. A familiar is often sent by a mentor and is more than a pet. While it could be a pet, the familiar is sent to help with the metaphysical connection, and there is a deep, unexplainable bond.

Relationships with the spirits of animals could fall into chapter 1 on Spirit Guides or chapter 3 on Loved Ones. The point is to realize that the animal kingdom is all around us as spirits.

These animal spirits represent the collective unconscious, which Carl Jung described as everyone being linked through the unconscious mind.[10] This explanation means that an animal spirit such as Wolf carries the inherited characteristics of the entire species in addition to the traits of an individual wolf. Therefore, if we have an animal guide of a particular species, for example Wolf, it has general characteristics associated with it, such as leader or teacher, and a willingness to stand alone when necessary.

Still, there may also be unique attributes of the particular animal spirit that works with us. For example, while a Wolf guide might have distinguishing physical characteristics, it might be an alpha male or alpha female or a different, more docile member of the pack. The point is the animal that comes to you will have the characteristics you need.

IDENTIFYING

Animal guides are easy to identify once you pay attention. They may have always been your favorite animal. If you love lions, then Lion is probably a guide to you. You also may encounter an animal guide in your dreams.

....

9. Wilhelm Wundt, *Element der Volkerpscholologie: Entwicklungsgeschichte Der Menschheit,* 1912 (Whitefish, MT: Kessinger Publishing, LLC 2010), 116.

10. C.G. Jung, *Two Essays on Analytical Psychology* (Collected Works of C.G. Jung, Volume 7), "The Structure of the Unconscious" (Princeton: Princeton University Press, 1972), pp. 263–292; C.G. Jung, *Structure and Dynamics of the Psyche* (Collected Works of C.G. Jung, Volume 8), "The Significance of Constitution and Heredity in Psychology" (Princeton: Princeton University Press, 1970), pp. 229–230.

I dreamed of giant robot-like mosquitos almost every night when I was young. Mosquitos are giant in Texas, and they can annoy you. Their bites itch like crazy, so they get your attention. My head was always in the clouds when I was little, and I needed to pay attention. They are the guides to whip me into shape when I need to pay attention. They also remind me not to get so irritated by the little things in life and not to be so hard on myself. But a mosquito!? You see, we all want the *impressive* guides. I get a mosquito from my dreams! Well, Mosquito was the animal spirit I needed my whole life.

Another way you might identify an animal spirit is to see the animal over and over. While this may be a sign sent to us from an animal messenger, this also may be an animal spirit guide.

Another thing to be aware of is that animals have spirits that live on after they pass from their physical form. Just as humans return to visit, it is not unusual for animals to return as well, appearing in spirit/ghost form. The sightings of animal ghosts are widespread and not limited to any particular species.

CONNECTING

Always remember that the animal spirits dwell in your unconscious mind, waiting for you to discover them, but they have been there all along. The best way to connect with an animal spirit is to spend time in nature or go anywhere the animal you want to connect with would have liked when they were in physical form. Spending time in their habitat will help you adjust your vibrational frequency to that of the animal.

Whether you can see or sense an animal or talk to it, be respectful of the animal's space and territory. Let it come closer to you. Do not rush at it. Learn about the animal. By this, I mean the actual animal you encounter—hold off going straight to a guidebook and instead take note of any observations you can make. This restraint will help you pick up on the individual characteristics of the particular animal. Once you have done this, it is excellent to consult a guidebook to gain additional insights and confirm your impressions, but it is essential to see what you learn and feel instead of what someone tells you.

Practice
11 Ways to Recognize
Animal Guides in Your Life

The following will help you identify your animal guides and animals in spirit. Once you have identified them, you can connect with them by meditating, journaling, and spending time with them in any way that is realistic to do so. In addition, this list will help you ascertain if perhaps you are already consistently working with an animal guide or recognizing if one is trying to get your attention.

1. You have always thought about them since you were little.
2. They are the first animal you want to go see when you enter a zoo.
3. They appear to you in person, often out of the blue.
4. They appear to you in movies.
5. You see them in the clouds.
6. You see them on signs, buildings, trucks, etc.
7. You hear them mentioned in passing or in songs.
8. You dream about them.
9. They meet you in meditations.
10. A psychic mentions them to you.
11. You use pendulums or cards to identify them.

PROTECTING

Most animals choose to be pure of heart, and you need no protection, but there are stories of animals that decide to do the bidding of lower vibrations. Animals have a choice, just like any other spirit. For example, a dog can choose its frequency to vibrate, just as a snake can. It is not so much about which animal type is typically considered dangerous or feared; it is more about the individual within the collective of that animal species. For example, a dog may choose a vibration that does not vibe with you or vice versa.

Our law and medicine class took a field trip to Parkland Hospital in Dallas, Texas. We observed autopsies and visited children with the highest level of trauma. There was a young boy there at the time who was from my hometown. I had heard his story from my parents because it was all over the news: A dog had attacked him and he was mauled to the brink of death. I remember looking at the precious young boy through his protective glass encasement. His spirit hovered above his body, and I told a classmate he wasn't going to live. I remember getting a stare down for that. Indeed, the boy left that body three days later.

But what about the dog, I wondered? As it turns out, the dog was abused by its owners and forced to fight. I have often thought that all animals are innocent, and it is our job to protect them. I do believe we should treat all animals with kindness and respect. Still, I think it is a somewhat condescending, superior viewpoint to assume animals cannot choose how to respond to their experiences.

For one thing, animals protect us every bit as much or perhaps more so than we defend them. This protection of us is a choice they make. They are subject to the same *fight or flight* responses that humans are, which is why some abused animals *choose* to become aggressive bullies while others become submissive and cowed.

COLLABORATING

Animals are great collaborators. Many have helped us survive by helping us farm our ancestral land or give us a better means of travel. Most animals can also collaborate with us in the spirit sense. They can carry out tasks for us and spread information to others in the animal realms. They often serve as messengers for us from other spirits. Also, remember that perhaps we are meant to serve as spirit guides to the animals. Birds love to collaborate with you to send you messages from your loved ones.

When Mary's mother-in-law passed away, all the children and their spouses planned her service at the funeral home. As they walked out of the funeral home a male and female cardinal were sitting on the fence in the parking lot. Everyone immediately commented how their mom was together with their dad. The cardinals were a source of comfort for the entire family. Now cardinals show up for Mary every time she needs to know someone has her back or she feels lonely. A reader validated this for Mary by telling her that the people she considered cardinals are with her and love her.

Another bird that shows up for Mary is the blue jay. One day she was walking her dogs and having a particularly hard time in life. She asked her mom for a sign and immediately saw a blue jay sitting in the tree staring at her. One day she was her way to a job interview and before she pulled out of the parking lot there was a blue jay staring at her from a tree. She nailed the interview and got the job. Now every time she sees a blue jay she simply says, *thanks Mom, I love you too.*

Practice
Groupings of Animal Guides
According to Ways They Can Help You

The following practice will help you find animal guides to help you with certain needs in your life. Read through this list to see which attributes might help you at this time. Then choose which animal you associate with that attribute and appeals most to you to work with as a guide. You may also select several features and guides, or even use them to create a hybrid guide. I recommend choosing three attributes and seeing which animals overlap or repeat.

Try to leave your biases behind. Remember that no animal is better than another and even animals that strike fear in you may turn out to be the guide you need at this time. They will help you with shadow work you want to avoid.

Animals you have not been drawn to before may be the very ones you need in order to deal with an issue in your life at this time. Perhaps pick the one you know the least about and get to know them. The spirits of all animals are fascinating.

It is helpful to find ways to remember your guide. For example, you can use photos or talismans. If you decide to have a hybrid guide, you can sketch it or take the animals' pictures and make them into a collage. Go as deep into your work and research as you feel led.

- **Abundance**—Buffalo, Cow, Dragon, Kangaroo, Ladybug, Lobster, Locust, Mouse, Pelican, Pig, Puffin
- **Action**—Badger, Beaver, Bee, Caterpillar, Gazelle, Iguana, Quail, Rabbit, Reindeer, Roadrunner, Squirrel
- **Adaptability**—Blue Jay, Catfish, Chameleon, Cheetah, Hummingbird, Kangaroo, Komodo Dragon, Octopus, Puffin, Raccoon, Seahorse

- **Alchemy (Magick)**—Cat, Caterpillar, Dragonfly, Frog, Fox, Owl, Raven, Snake, Spider, Swan, Unicorn
- **Anxiety, Calming**—Angelfish, Cricket, Deer, Gazelle, Hippopotamus, Koala, Koi, Puffin, Sloth, Squirrel, Turtle
- **Astral Projection**—Butterfly, Crane, Horse, Jackal, Locust, Loon, Pelican, Penguin, Reindeer, Sasquatch, Whale
- **Awakening**—Elk, Butterfly, Firefly, Ibis, Jackal, Koi, Lobster, Moth, Phoenix, Polar Bear, Praying Mantis
- **Balance**—Angelfish, Canary, Chicken, Crane, Flamingo, Gazelle, Jaguar, Koi, Raccoon, Seal, Woodpecker
- **Boundaries**—Armadillo, Bear, Bull, Chimpanzee, Donkey, Dragon, Hyena, Rhinoceros, Shark, Spider, Wolf
- **Challenges**—Aardvark, Badger, Buffalo, Crow, Jellyfish, Komodo Dragon, Locust, Loon, Meerkat, Salmon, Tiger
- **Changes**—Butterfly, Catfish, Cricket, Cuckoo, Electric Eel, Lizard, Monkey, Phoenix, Pig, Snake, Squirrel
- **Communication**—Blue Jay, Catfish, Chimpanzee, Cricket, Crow, Dolphin, Hyena, Mockingbird, Swan, Whale, Wolf
- **Communication with Spirits**—Cat, Dragonfly, Eagle, Hippopotamus, Ibis, Leopard, Moth, Opossum, Oriole, Unicorn, Woodpecker
- **Community**—Ant, Bat, Bee, Buffalo, Dog, Elk, Hyena, Monkey, Moose, Prairie Dog, Wolf
- **Confidence**—Alligator, Bear, Boar, Bobcat, Bull, Cheetah, Mouse, Oriole, Peacock, Penguin, Tiger
- **Courage**—Bear, Bull, Chicken, Fox, Hawk, Komodo Dragon, Lion, Polar Bear, Porcupine, Raccoon, Sparrow
- **Creativity**—Blue Jay, Buffalo, Cricket, Fox, Locust, Octopus, Rabbit, Raccoon, Seal, Spider, Unicorn
- **Death**—Dove, Ibis, Jackal, Jaguar, Moose, Owl, Polar Bear, Raven, Scorpion, Sphinx, Vulture
- **Decisions**—Blue Jay, Chameleon, Coyote, Donkey, Fox, Gazelle, Ostrich, Rabbit, Raccoon, Rhinoceros, Spider
- **Details (Methodical Action)**—Ant, Beaver, Bee, Caterpillar, Iguana, Meerkat, Mouse, Spider, Termite, Wasp, Zebra

- **Diversity**—Chameleon, Clownfish, Kiwi, Lizard, Octopus, Opossum, Salamander, Seahorse, Sphinx, Spider, Zebra
- **Dreams**—Beaver, Coyote, Dragonfly, Giraffe, Jackal, Lizard, Penguin, Polar Bear, Raven, Seal, Unicorn
- **Empathy**—Armadillo, Cardinal, Catfish, Cheetah, Chimpanzee, Dog, Dolphin, Gorilla, Horse, Koala, Starfish
- **Family**—Bear, Beaver, Gorilla, Kangaroo, Ladybug, Mockingbird, Monkey, Otter, Pig, Whale, Wolf
- **Fertility**—Beetle, Bull, Chicken, Earthworm, Electric Eel, Elephant, Frog, Rabbit, Sparrow
- **Focus**—Camel, Cardinal, Crane, Donkey, Hawk, Lemur, Mouse, Octopus, Praying Mantis, Shark, Tiger
- **Forgiveness**—Angelfish, Canary, Dog, Firefly, Jellyfish, Koi, Ladybug, Manatee, Pelican, Penguin, Robin
- **Frequency Alignment (other dimensions and spirits)**—Bat, Buffalo, Butterfly, Clownfish, Crane, Firefly, Hummingbird, Mockingbird, Panda, Sasquatch, Sparrow
- **Friendship**—Bluebird, Chickadee, Chimpanzee, Dog, Dolphin, Giraffe, Horse, Meerkat, Otter, Reindeer, Seagull
- **Good Fortune**—Albatross, Chickadee, Cricket, Frog, Goldfish, Koi, Ladybug, Lizard, Pig, Seal, Stork
- **Grace**—Albatross, Angelfish, Deer, Eagle, Gazelle, Giraffe, Hippopotamus, Jaguar, Manatee, Peacock, Swan
- **Grief**—Bluebird, Chimpanzee, Deer, Dove, Jackal, Moth, Polar Bear, Robin, Scorpion, Sparrow, Woodpecker
- **Grounding**—Alligator, Badger, Boar, Cheetah, Gorilla, Hippopotamus, Jaguar, Mouse, Ostrich, Praying Mantis, Quail
- **Harmony**—Angelfish, Deer, Dove, Goldfish, Koala, Koi, Panda, Reindeer, Robin, Starfish, Turtle
- **Healing**—Albatross, Badger, Canary, Cow, Cuckoo, Flamingo, Iguana, Koala, Phoenix, Scorpion, Snake
- **Honor**—Alligator, Elephant, Elk, Gorilla, Kangaroo, Lion, Monkey, Salmon, Swan, Woodpecker
- **Humor**—Clownfish, Coyote, Dolphin, Hyena, Kiwi, Lemur, Meerkat, Monkey, Otter, Puffin, Squirrel

- **Independence**—Aardvark, Albatross, Bobcat, Canary, Cat, Leopard, Lizard, Moose, Praying Mantis, Rhinoceros, Shark
- **Intelligence**—Blue Jay, Donkey, Fox, Gorilla, Lemur, Magpie, Mockingbird, Octopus, Pig, Seal, Wolf
- **Intuition**—Catfish, Chameleon, Chimpanzee, Flamingo, Giraffe, Jellyfish, Lizard, Locust, Magpie, Rabbit, Whale
- **Joy**—Canary, Chickadee, Cuckoo, Goldfish, Hummingbird, Ladybug, Lemur, Oriole, Otter, Seagull, Sparrow
- **Leadership**—Beaver, Cardinal, Dragon, Eagle, Elephant, Horse, Kiwi, Lion, Moose, Reindeer, Shark
- **Love**—Angelfish, Bluebird, Cow, Dove, Flamingo, Hummingbird, Manatee, Peacock, Rabbit, Seal, Swan
- **Loyalty**—Bluebird, Blue Jay, Bull, Dog, Earthworm, Elephant, Gorilla, Hippopotamus, Horse, Kiwi, Lion, Salmon
- **Magic**—Cat, Crow, Dragonfly, Ibis, Octopus, Owl, Raven, Starfish, Unicorn, Zebra
- **Manifestation**—Badger, Beetle, Buffalo, Crow, Dragon, Electric Eel, Firefly, Ladybug, Magpie, Pig, Sparrow
- **Metamorphosis**—Butterfly, Caterpillar, Dragonfly, Frog, Phoenix, Praying Mantis, Salamander, Sphinx, Starfish, Termite, Wasp
- **Motivation**—Ant, Boar, Canary, Donkey, Firefly, Locust, Mouse, Roadrunner, Squirrel, Stork, Woodpecker
- **Past Lives**—Beetle, Ibis, Leopard, Oriole, Phoenix, Polar Bear, Praying Mantis, Salamander, Sasquatch, Sphinx, Vulture
- **Patience**—Alligator, Badger, Camel, Chameleon, Chicken, Hyena, Komodo Dragon, Penguin, Rhinoceros, Seahorse, Tiger
- **Peace**—Clownfish, Deer, Dove, Giraffe, Jellyfish, Koala, Loon, Manatee, Puffin, Sloth, Whale
- **Perspective**—Eagle, Firefly, Hawk, Hippopotamus, Iguana, Kiwi, Mole, Seagull, Seahorse, Sloth, Zebra
- **Playfulness**—Bobcat, Cuckoo, Dog, Fox, Goldfish, Lemur, Meerkat, Otter, Roadrunner, Skunk, Squirrel
- **Positive Outlook**—Dolphin, Hummingbird, Ladybug, Ostrich, Pelican, Prairie Dog, Puffin, Quail, Robin, Salmon, Starfish

- **Purpose**—Aardvark, Albatross, Beetle, Donkey, Dragon, Earthworm, Flamingo, Mole, Mongoose, Tiger, Vulture
- **Protection**—Armadillo, Bear, Camel, Cow, Hippopotamus, Jellyfish, Kangaroo, Lobster, Mockingbird, Mongoose, Opossum
- **Respect**—Cardinal, Cow, Gorilla, Jaguar, Kiwi, Panda, Seagull, Skunk, Stork, Turtle, Wolf
- **Self-Worth**—Armadillo, Boar, Cheetah, Lion, Magpie, Mongoose, Moose, Oriole, Peacock, Roadrunner, Skunk
- **Sensuality**—Albatross, Cat, Elk, Goldfish, Leopard, Lobster, Moth, Peacock, Salmon, Skunk, Tiger
- **Sexuality/Gender**—Chicken, Clownfish, Deer, Earthworm, Frog, Komodo Dragon, Penguin, Seahorse, Shark, Starfish, Zebra
- **Shadows**—Bat, Electric Eel, Jackal, Jaguar, Lobster, Loon, Magpie, Mongoose, Moth, Salamander, Sasquatch
- **Shape-shifting**—Bat, Cat, Coyote, Crow, Flamingo, Lemur, Leopard, Owl, Raven, Sasquatch, Shark
- **Success**—Chickadee, Iguana, Magpie, Mongoose, Monkey, Panda, Rhinoceros, Roadrunner, Snake, Stork, Termite, Turtle
- **Survival**—Aardvark, Alligator, Bluebird, Bobcat, Camel, Cardinal, Catfish, Chameleon, Clownfish, Scorpion, Seagull
- **Teamwork**—Ant, Beaver, Bee, Coyote, Hyena, Meerkat, Prairie Dog, Reindeer, Salmon, Termite, Wasp
- **Temperance**—Camel, Cheetah, Elephant, Mongoose, Opossum, Panda, Sloth, Sphinx, Stork, Turtle, Vulture
- **Tenacity**—Aardvark, Ant, Boar, Bobcat, Bull, Crane, Cuckoo, Iguana, Komodo Dragon, Scorpion, Seahorse
- **Tolerance**—Dragon, Hawk, Loon, Manatee, Mole, Rhinoceros, Seagull, Skunk, Turtle, Unicorn, Vulture
- **Transformation**—Aardvark, Beetle, Camel, Caterpillar, Chickadee, Electric Eel, Frog, Ibis, Raccoon, Salamander, Swan
- **Transmutation**—Bat, Butterfly, Caterpillar, Crow, Dragonfly, Gazelle, Lobster, Phoenix, Scorpion, Snake
- **Trust**—Armadillo, Coyote, Cuckoo, Jellyfish, Koala, Manatee, Mole, Moth, Opossum, Porcupine, Vulture

- **Truth**—Armadillo, Boar, Chickadee, Cow, Dolphin, Dove, Earthworm, Hawk, Ostrich, Panda, Stork
- **Vibration**—Bat, Cricket, Dolphin, Earthworm, Elephant, Hummingbird, Loon, Mole, Sasquatch, Woodpecker, Whale
- **Vision**—Bluebird, Bobcat, Eagle, Giraffe, Hawk, Leopard, Mole, Oriole, Owl, Peacock, Salamander
- **Vitality**—Ant, Cardinal, Electric Eel, Elk, Goldfish, Horse, Kangaroo, Otter, Rhinoceros, Roadrunner, Skunk
- **Wisdom**—Alligator, Beetle, Crane, Elk, Lion, Mockingbird, Moose, Owl, Opossum, Snake, Sphinx

HONORING

Animal guides should always be honored. They appreciate gifts of food, sparkly items, or other safe treats left out for them. One way to honor them is by having photos of them or carved statues that you wear or place in your home. The best way to honor them is to take care of the environment in which they live and fight for their rights when they cannot fight for themselves.

DEMYSTIFYING

I have often heard it said that animal guides cannot be reincarnated people or reincarnated pets. The reason given revolves around what I refer to as the reincarnation video game theory. Many teachings have evolved from Hindu teachings and turned into a loose reincarnation belief that goes something like this: We come to Earth to learn lessons. When we die, we will reincarnate according to the lessons we have learned. Some even believe that you will reincarnate as an animal if your karma was not up to snuff.

Well, for many of us, we are beginning to know that while we may choose to incarnate here, and while it may be for some lessons, we are also here merely for the experience. Not everything is about a lesson or how to get to the next level on the video game of life. Let me be clear: Animal guides can be reincarnated people or reincarnated pets. A person does not reincarnate as an animal as a punishment. It is a choice. Many people would love to live the life of a cat. Animals are beautiful spirits that are no longer under old, outmoded paradigm thinking.

6
Elementals

A tree stands alone in the median of a motorway in County Clare, Ireland. There is a fence around it. The tree is messy and overgrown, and to many eyes unattractive, so you might find it strange to see it singled out in such a manner. But this is Ireland. And no place in the world seems to be more connected to Mother Earth and the elementals.

This messy tree whose branches obscure its trunk is a Hawthorn tree, and Hawthorn trees are known to be places where the faeries hang out. In the middle of a motorway in Ireland, this tree is particularly important to the faeries. This Hawthorn is the tree where warring faeries, the Kerry Faeries and the Connacht Faeries, hold their battles. When the roadway was first under construction, many people were convinced that if the tree were to be cut down, damaged in any way, or even relocated, there could be terrible consequences. These consequences would befall anyone involved in the project and possibly even the motorists who later drove by on the motorway.

As it turns out, the local government took the situation seriously too. The rumor is they were afraid to take the chance of angering the faerie realm. So, despite the additional costs, they chose to establish a five-meter perimeter (approximately fifteen feet) around the Hawthorn on all sides, surround it with a barrier fence, and then reroute the planned roadway around the bush.[11]

In my opinion, it is a beautiful thing that the people of Ireland have not forgotten their connection to Mother Earth and the elementals. They continue to respect and honor them and possibly even fear them a little bit as well. There is a supplement to this particular story, however. Several years after the roadway completion, someone in the dead of night took a chainsaw to the tree. To the horror of the locals, the culprit cut off all the Hawthorn's branches, leaving only its trunk. People assumed that the

. . . .
11. Gordon Deegan, "Fairy Bush Survives the Motorway Planners," *The Irish Times*, 29 May 1999, www.irishtimes.com/news/fairy-bush-survives-the -motorway-planners-1.190053, accessed November 20, 2021.

tree was dead and that there were likely frightening repercussions soon to come. However, within months, the Hawthorn was back, nearly to its former glory. Today, it is still messy and chaotic and sending a clear message about who has the upper hand in this situation. The police investigated the chainsaw massacre but to no apparent avail. However, do not despair thinking the culprit got away with it and went unpunished. My money is on the faeries!

I have found this story fascinating for quite some time for several reasons. First, as someone in touch with the value of all energy, the tree itself holds special meaning for me. When you add in the elementals (faeries) gathered there, its value magnifies. Also, as a lawyer representing construction companies, I know how much is at stake when construction comes to a complete standstill. For this to have occurred, despite their denials later, those involved honestly did believe in the power of the elementals.

On a more personal note, even though I never really considered myself a *tree hugger*, I've come to realize that I am one in a different kind of way. During the winter of 2021 in Texas, where I live, there was a nasty ice storm. About two weeks after the ice storm, I realized the tree outside my bedroom balcony had been a casualty and was now *dead*. However, interestingly, I began to receive messages of great comfort from this tree, more and more as time went on. I had never really paid attention to the tree before the ice storm except to notice squirrels playing in its branches. However, I became acutely aware that I had bonded with this tree more when it was dead than I ever did while it was alive. This bonding made me realize something essential. The life force energy of all beings, even trees, lives on after death, and you can communicate with it. This tree had been a living part of nature and the elemental kingdom and was truly no different than any other form that energy may take. Therefore, I was able to communicate with it in a way that ended up serving us both.

THE FLIP SIDE

I have encountered an elemental in human form that I absolutely know was a siren. It is interesting because I never really believed in sirens until I met one and dealt with her. In Greek mythology, sirens were extremely dangerous. They lived in deep ocean waters and would lure sailors to shipwreck by singing enchanting music. Initially characterized as women and birds, they eventually were described more like mermaids.

The siren I encountered was straight-up an enchantress. She could lull you with her words, and her magic was strong. Typical of sirens, she was petite and had strawberry blonde hair. However, because I can so easily see spirits, I often was able to catch glimpses of her true form. Her teeth were almost that of a vampire's teeth. But she lured people in, and then used them for her purposes. I have no doubt this was a modern-day siren, an elemental that moved within my inner circle for quite some time, wreaking havoc while in disguise.

INTRODUCING

Nature spirits, including the elementals, are believed to be various types of beings or spirits that inhabit nature. The belief in their existence was almost universal in the ancient era of religions that embodied animism, the idea that everything has a soul. This thinking still exists among people who believe that all things possess life, especially amid many occultists and neo-pagan witches.

When Christianity entered the picture, it had a hard time overcoming the idea of the ancient gods. Monotheism was just not conceivable to the people of that time. Therefore, many of the pagan beliefs were folded into Christianity with angels and saints. The difficulty came in how to handle the elementals. The elementals were not easily integrated, so it was easier to demonize them.

Literature has bolstered the concept of nature spirits with engaging characters such as Puck in Shakespeare's *A Midsummer Night's Dream* and Tinker Bell in James Barrie's *Peter Pan*. These are just two examples of countless other tales of nature spirits mentioned in books and stories passed down through the ages. The belief in and the resulting folklore and mythology surrounding nature spirits are not limited to any culture. Legends abound in all areas of the world.

Nature spirits possess supernatural powers and are typically invisible to most humans, except those with the psychic ability of clairvoyance. However, I hope to change that thinking by getting you to realize that all kinds of spirits are all around us all the time, and they are just as real as we are. For that reason, anyone can sense them if they want to and are willing to dedicate the time to learn how to do so. It's just a matter of opening up your mind and redefining what it means to be psychic.

IDENTIFYING

The four physical elements of fire, earth, air, and water (as well as the fifth element, spirit or ether) each have spirits associated with them that dwell in the physical plane. Some of us can see them, but most humans, especially in the West, are unaware of how real these spirits are. People opined that elementals were spirits from some other plane throughout time because they are not human like us. I disagree with this argument and believe instead that energy can choose its form and does. The determining factor is not what spirits were created to be but rather what they choose to be. In fact, once we realize we are all just energy that can change form, we will realize that any being can, in theory, choose any form of beingness. Elementals may share some of the characteristics of humans, but their primary (chosen) purpose is to help protect and heal Gaia or Mother Earth.

Each physical element has a broad catchall name for their particular elementals, but other spirits can align with that element. For example, gnomes are associated with earth, salamanders are associated with fire, sylphs are associated with air, and undines are associated with water. However, the world of elementals is extraordinarily diverse, and there are many more types of spirits associated with each element than we can discuss here. Also, it is useless to try to pigeonhole them. As soon as you try to generalize about them, they will try to prove you wrong!

The earth is the cornerstone element and provides the solid foundation for our physical plane. It nurtures us by providing us with the air we breathe, the food we eat, the water we drink, and everything else that enables us to thrive abundantly.

Earth elementals come in many forms, including the crystals born deep inside Mother Earth. These beautiful creations are magical beings in and of themselves. Other earth elementals include spirits called gnomes. Gnome derives from the Greek *genomus,* meaning earth dweller. They work with trees, flowers, minerals, rocks, crystals, and living things such as animals because they are so close in vibration to the earth. The gnomes have more names, such as brownies, dryads, durdalis, elves, hamadryads, pans, pixies, pygmies, sylvestres, and satyrs. Perhaps the most famous of the earth elementals are the Irish leprechauns. They are dressed in green, reported to be about three feet tall, old and temperamental, and hoarders of their treasure. Also well-known are the dwarves who guard the earth's minerals, inhabit mines and caves, and efficiently move through the earth.

The element of water provides purification and connects us to our subconscious. All water spirits are undines. The word *undine* means wave in Greek. Undines, or water faeries, watch over bodies of water and even direct the flow and course the water takes on Earth.

Just as water has many various forms such as mist, steam, humidity, puddles, streams, rivers, lakes, and oceans, there are also countless forms of water spirits. They work tirelessly against killing sea creatures for sport and polluting the oceans, streams, and rivers. Because water relates to our emotions and unconscious mind, so do the water faeries, and they understand how water's movements affect other spirits and our human feelings.

Mermaids, sea maids, naiads, selkies, oceanid, ningyos, and potamides are all undines. They reside in coral caves, lakes, rivers, seas, marshlands, waterfalls, fountains, and beneath lily pads. Beauty and grace seem to be critical aspects of most water spirits. Since water has typically been a feminine element, most water spirits are seen with feminine and human characteristics.

The fire element is both destructive and creative simultaneously, which is why it is associated with transformation. All the spirits of fire in this world are typically classified as salamanders. Fire would be non-existent without these beings, as their presence is needed to even light just matches. They also work through our liver, bloodstream, and emotions and help to keep us warm. These spirits are highly knowledgeable and proficient with magic. They always need feeding and absorb outside energy to fuel their power. They can reside anywhere, and they appear within tongues of fire or may appear as fiery balls and peer into houses or run over fields.

The air element governs our communication—our thoughts and breath of life. Air is like spirit in many ways. (Remember, the word spirit means breath.) Air is the element that carries the energetic signals and frequencies from which our senses receive information. Sylphs are the spirits of the air. They are mischievous, swift, clever, and unpredictable faeries. Sylphs are also called silfides. They can control the weather and anything else relating to the earth and sky. They have the highest vibrations among the four elementals. Air is the mind and intellect element, so they are sometimes responsible for inspiring art and inventions. Air faeries get us thinking, communicating, and laughing. Their primary habitat is the tops of the mountains.

Compared to the other elementals, sylphs are often considered the most beautiful. They usually have wings and appear like a crossbreed of an angel and a faery. However, they can also assume human form. When the ancients believed that sylphs lived in the element of air, they were not referring to Earth's natural atmosphere per se, but to the invisible, intangible, spiritual medium of *air*—an ethereal substance similar in composition but far more subtle.

CONNECTING

Elementals (or nature spirits) usually abide in trees, rivers, plants, bogs, mountains, underground, and inside minerals. They attach themselves to practically every natural thing. In China, for example, they watch over the rice, silk, roads, and gateways. The Shinto religion of Japan worships all aspects of nature, its forces, and its spirits. The Greeks and Romans also practiced the worship of nature spirits, who believed spirits inhabited every glen, pool, and even the air. As you can see, nature spirits have been acknowledged, respected, and even worshipped universally throughout time.

It is typically assumed that elementals live in their elemental realm. They seem to be entities that are closely associated with a specific place or location. It is also thought this type of creature resides in a realm that is either above or below our level of perception. Perception is defined as that which can be perceived through the normal five senses. However, this is a limiting construct. Spirits, including nature spirits and elementals, are around us all the time. We only need to adjust our frequency to perceive them.

The wings of an insect in flight are impossible for the human eye to perceive as more than a blur. There are many sounds animals can hear that humans cannot because the frequency of the sound is outside the range of our perception. Just because our eyes cannot see insects' wings or our ears cannot hear the sound of a dog whistle, it does not mean those things do not exist. If captured on a video or audio recording, you can adjust the recording's speed/vibration/frequency and see or hear these things that otherwise are inaccessible to us using our *ordinary* senses. Please believe me when I tell you that there are so many other things that exist outside our *standard range of human perception* that it will simply boggle your mind!

While all spirits are at frequencies our ordinary human senses have difficulty perceiving, it is challenging to interact with elementals because they tend to steer clear of us. We have given them plenty of reasons not to trust us and to avoid us at all costs, but gnomes will usually comply if we try to establish a connection with them.

Gnomes typically look like humans, except for those who live in tiny streams and ponds. Those gnomes are a shimmering green or blue and are beautiful, graceful, and highly emotional. Undines (water faeries) are known as friendly and approachable spirits that gladly work with humans. The fire salamanders, while erratic and intense, are open to helping humans as well.

The air sylphs are believed to leave astonishing green faery rings in meadows and fields, leaving evidence for us that they danced in circles as they passed by. I once sat in such a ring just before giving a crystal presentation and could feel how the ring blessed every one of the crystals I had brought with me. I was then inspired to gift the crystals to a room of sixty people. It was magical. These playful sylphs are said to be sympathetic towards humans and can inspire us with significant creative ideas.

Since elementals can be somewhat temperamental, a few suggestions on connecting with them may be helpful. First, keep an open mind. It very much helps to open your mind to the possibility that wonders exist beyond what you can see and hear with your physical eyes and ears. An open mind heightens your awareness of elementals and their willingness to reveal themselves to you.

Second, you must be respectful to their living environment. Spend time in their habitat or home but pay honor to it and ask for permission to enter. For instance, you can ask before you mow the lawn or cut the trees.

Third, invite them to hang out with you just as you would a human you want to get to know. Invite them over and treat them with hospitality. They love food and gifts.

Fourth, as with all spirits, meet them at their vibrational state.

Finally, adjust your frequency to the frequency of the element you are trying to get to know. To do this, remember the practice, 11 Steps to Broaden Your Frequency Bandwidth mentioned in chapter 1. You will want to use these steps but adjust them to the elemental with whom you are connecting.

Following are some examples of elementals and their frequency:

- **Earth Elementals**—They typically have grounded, dense energy. You will want your frequency to slow down and become steadier, even heavier, as you adjust your frequency to that of the earth elementals. Be sure to keep both your feet on the ground, and if your feet are bare, that is even better. The root chakra and everything associated with it will help you adjust to the Earth's elemental frequency. Some crystals to use include but are not limited to tiger's eye; smoky quartz; malachite; brown, black, or red agates and jaspers; green aventurine; jade; black tourmaline; calcite; jet.

- **Water Elementals**—They are connected to emotions and our subconscious thoughts. The frequency of water elementals is typically reached by quieting your mind and silencing the chatter. Even a few moments outside with eyes closed listening to the sounds of nature can help with this. If there are water sounds nearby, that will particularly help facilitate your connection. If you can't get outside, listening to a recording of flowing water while closing your eyes and quieting your mind is the next best thing. Crystals that assist you in reaching the frequency of the water elementals include but are not limited to halite, blue lace agate, moonstone, opal, aquamarine, larimar, chrysoprase, pearl, kunzite.

- **Air Elementals**—They are communicators and messengers and deal with intellect. Sound and vocal noises are possible only due to the vibration of the air. They may have a subtle vibration, but it is at a high frequency. To connect to the air elementals, it may be necessary to spend a little more time quieting your mind. If you have a meditation practice, trying to communicate to them immediately after meditation would be ideal. Being outdoors would help also but is not necessary. Be sure to set an evident intention before attempting to connect to the air elementals, and they will very likely oblige. Crystals that assist you include but are not limited to amethyst, blue topaz, lapis lazuli, iolite, labradorite, sodalite, blue kyanite, selenite.

- **Fire Elemental**—These are fast-acting beings of passion. The best way to connect to this element is by staring into a flame. An outdoor fire pit, campfire, or even a lantern or candle can facilitate this connection. If you don't have access to an outdoor setting, you can also stare into the flames of a fireplace. As well, a candle may suffice. Other ideas are watching and listening to video and audio recordings of a crackling fire. Finally, should you ever see a salamander, talk directly to it, and this can help you connect to the fire elementals. (Even envisioning talking to a salamander in your mind's eye can facilitate this type of communication.) Crystals that will assist in connection with this swift energy include but are not limited to fire agate, carnelian, citrine, ruby, amber, flint, sunstone, Apache tear.

Regarding the habitats of elementals and where best to connect with them, here is additional info and some suggestions: Gnomes are the earth's spirits and can be found in rocky places, but some reside in households. Dwarves are typically located around vacant mines. Trolls like bridges, caves, cliffs, and dark places. Faeries love the beauty in nature, such as areas with lots of trees and flowers. If you are trying to connect with elves, stick to forests and parks. If you attempt to connect to pixies, they can be found anywhere there is vegetation, even if the foliage is decomposing.

In general, to connect with any earth spirit, focus on your intention to meet them. You can touch the soil, tree, grass, rock, or any natural thing with which they are known to interact.

If you want to connect with water spirits—undines like water nymphs, mermaids, sand spirits, oceanids, and merrows—research about their preferred place of dwelling and meditate there. Water nymphs love streams, so focusing while on a rock in the middle of a stream would be a good start. Mermaids live in the sea while sand spirits like beaches, so meditating there would be ideal. While near the ocean, focus on your intention of connecting with the water elementals. Stare at the water and let the sounds of its waves wash over you. Feel its energy and work on feeling the energy of other spirits flowing with it. You can even touch the water as you concentrate.

Fire spirits—salamanders—are perhaps the hardest to find despite their presence almost everywhere. You can find them in hot places, or you can feel their presence anywhere. Focus on your goal of connecting with them and feel the fire burning in your heart and the heat of your body around you, then work on feeling their energies.

If you desire to connect with faeries of the air—sylphs—mountain tops and open spaces like the meadows or fields are their favorites. However, they are also present everywhere. To interact with them, meditate and invite them over.

Practice
11 Ways to Scry to Connect with Elementals

Scrying means to look into a medium (such as water or fire) to detect a message or vision for the past, present, or future. The following proposes various forms of scrying to help you connect with different elements.

1. Wave Scrying (water)—Watch and listen to the rise and fall of the waves.
2. Waterfall Scrying (water)—Listen through the waterfall to the sounds that come forth.
3. Shell Scrying (water)—Listen to the sound from the shell.
4. Smoke Scrying (fire)—Look for patterns and figures in the smoke.
5. Fire Scrying (fire)—Listen to the fire crackling and watch for patterns and figures in the flames.
6. Cloud Scrying (air)—Gaze at the clouds, watching for visions, shapes, and the direction and speed of the cloud movement.
7. Wind Scrying (air)—The easiest way is to listen to the wind in trees and leaves.
8. Tea or Coffee Leaf Scrying (earth)—Read the formation of the tea or coffee. (There is more about this later in this chapter.)
9. Earthworm Scrying (earth)—Place earthworms in rich soil and read the patterns they make.

10. Crystal Ball Scrying (earth)—Gaze into a transparent quartz sphere to see what visions and patterns are revealed to you.

11. Mirror Scrying—Gaze into a mirror.

Practice
11 Ways to Connect with
Elementals Using the Elements

The following helps you connect with elementals by using the elements to which they are affiliated.

1. Decide what type of elemental you want to connect with at this time.

2. Set your intention to adjust your frequency to that of the elemental more easily.

3. If the elemental is associated with water, such as a mermaid or sprite, get a crystal or reflective bowl and fill it with moon water and rose water. Moon water is water that has been charged under the moon, perhaps a full or new moon.

4. Look for light patterns reflected in the water.

5. Add essential oil to the water and look for patterns the oil and water make.

6. Drop herbs or flowers in the water and look for patterns.

7. Another option is to astral project yourself into the water. We discuss astral projection in chapter 10, but this change in your frequency will connect you to the space and time needed to meet the elemental.

8. If the elemental is associated with fire, such as a dragon or salamander, an open flame is all you need.

9. Soften your gaze as you look at the candle or the bonfire.

10. Look for figures or symbols in the flame.

11. If the elemental is associated with the earth, such as a gnome or a tree, coffee grounds or tea leaves are great for scrying.

Practice
11 Steps to Tea Scrying
(Tasseography or Tasseomancy)

The following gives you steps to scrying with tea. Similar steps may be used for scrying with coffee.

1. Pick out your favorite loose-leaf tea. (Loose black tea leaves are recommended for beginners. Do not use tea bags.)
2. Brew the tea.
3. Place the tea leaves directly into a light-colored teacup.
4. While the tea cools, reflect on your intentions and transfer your energy into the tea leaves.
5. When the water is cool enough, the querent (one asking questions) should begin sipping the tea and thinking about their question.
6. When about a tablespoon of liquid is left, the one reading the leaves should begin swirling and turning the cup about three times from left to right.
7. Next, the tea leaf reader should turn the cup over a saucer and leave it up upside down for about a minute and then rotate the cup three times.
8. Next turn the cup upright with the handle pointing south.
9. Now it is time to read the leaves. Begin to look for shapes in the leaf residue. Generally, there are five types of symbols: animals, letters, mythical beings, numbers, and objects. Use your intuition or the first thing that comes that comes to your mind when you see the different shapes and symbols. For example if the tea leaves formed the shape of a dragon, there might be a message regarding dragons as a totem or perhaps the fire element of dragons.
10. Now read the leaves relating to the handle. Tea leaves near the handle represent events directly surrounding the querent. Tea leaves across from the handle represent outside influences.
11. Finally, the cup is divided into three sections. The rim is the present, the sides are the near future, and the bottom of the cup are the distant future.

PROTECTING

Make no mistake—elemental spirits can be dangerous. You do not want to anger them. Humans have angered them by not taking care of Earth. Every aspect of Earth is their home, and they are intent on taking care of her. Elemental spirits of this world, while generally helpful and crucial to nature and all living beings, can also be evil. This evil nature could be because they are triggered by the actions of specific humans and feel like they have to defend nature or themselves. Some are naturally malicious, and others have progressed into hostility because of all the negativity around them.

Some claim that all elementals have an amiable disposition, but not everyone agrees. There are many accounts of elementals with a tricky and malicious nature. They can be challenging to manage and potentially treacherous. Most agree, however, that when their confidence is won, they are faithful and true.

Those of the ancient world were taught how to communicate with these mysterious little people. Gaining their cooperation was of utmost importance, but ancient people were always warned never to betray the trust of the elementals, for if they did, the consequences could be dire. The invisible creatures, working through the subjective nature of man, could cause endless sorrow and probably ultimate destruction. So long as one helped others, the elementals would help him, but if he sought to use their aid selfishly to gain temporal power, they would turn upon him with unrelenting fury. The same was true if he desired to deceive them.

Swiss philosopher Paracelsus differed somewhat from the Greek mystics concerning the environmental limitations imposed on the nature spirits. Paracelsus constituted them of subtle, invisible ethers. According to this hypothesis, they would be visible only at certain times and only to those in sync with their ethereal vibrations. On the other hand, the Greeks believed that many nature spirits had material constitutions capable of functioning in the physical world. The difficulty of accurately judging the end of physical sight and the beginning of ethereal vision may account for these differences of opinion.

The best thing you can do to protect yourself from their wrath is to care for their habitat. You can also offer them gifts, which we cover in how to honor and appreciate them.

COLLABORATING

The elementals are excellent to collaborate with as long as you stay on their good side. They will help you organize your house, get your emotions in check, ground yourself, find things you are missing (but they may have hidden them), and anything else you can think of in your life. So, if you need a little fun in your life—let's be honest, we all do—then look no further than the elementals.

Practice
11 Ways to Collaborate with Elementals

The following gives ways to collaborate with the elementals. In the process, you will probably help out the Earth and find yourself having fun doing it.

1. Clean up your surroundings.
2. Recycle your waste.
3. Plant a tree.
4. Help with ocean life.
5. Design a faerie garden.
6. Play! Elementals love to have fun, and this brings life to the whole area where you play.
7. Warn the elementals before you cut down their homes such as trees or bushes, even before you mow your yard.
8. Hang crystals or prisms outside so they catch the light.
9. Build a faerie house.
10. Put out lots of little doors—faeries especially love them.
11. Perform energy healing on the Earth or parts of it. A crystal grid (grouping of crystals with intention) will also help you collaborate to heal the Earth and the elementals.

HONORING

You must honor and show appreciation to the elementals. They love gifts and food and provide all kinds of help in the home environment. Elementals love doorways, crystal balls, rainbow lights, coins, offering plates, and anything shiny.

DEMYSTIFYING

It has been said that elementals do not like to be called faeries. While that may have been true for a long time and still may be true in certain countries, I know for a fact that if you are respectful to them, they are fine with being called "faerie." These things are much more important to the academics who write about them than to the spirits themselves. Some of them also want to connect with you much more than many have historically claimed.

7
Disincarnates (Ghosts)

When the tragedy of Hurricane Katrina first hit the news, I became glued to the internet for information. Every second I could, I was watching or listening to the events surrounding the tragedy. It was devastating.

Some years later, I traveled with a medium friend and some others to New Orleans. I had visited New Orleans many times before Katrina, but not since the tragedy. We were there for a conference and did a lot of sightseeing.

As in every town I visit, I love to go to all the local spiritual shops. We visited the hoodoo shops and other local attractions. I was stunned when my husband pointed out how small the levies were that I had heard so much about on the news. The whole trip, I just thought about the souls who did not escape Katrina and the souls who were still lingering in New Orleans. I had and still have nothing but compassion for those souls. It broke my heart to think of them and it still does.

As the trip progressed, I became more and more tired. I wondered if I was a little sick or just exhausted. But it was a great trip with my husband and friends, so I didn't overthink it.

About a week after I got back to Dallas, I could barely wake up. I felt as if I was carrying fifty-pound weights around with me. I was in my office one day, and it hit me. Some new friends in spirit had attached to me and had come with me back to Texas. As much compassion as I had, and still have for these souls, I knew I did not have the energy to carry them around.

I explained the situation to four energy workers at my store. The energy workers and I gathered in my room and formed a circle. We explained to the souls that they were safe now and that others in spirit loved them and were waiting to show them just as much compassion as I had shown them. Five of the souls were convinced relatively quickly, and I felt much lighter. The other energy workers thought I would be fine.

I emphatically let them know that there was one more, and he did not want to leave. He was angry at God and everyone else for how he and the town had been treated. He said he wanted nothing to do with crossing to another situation where they did not care. He also stated he would go to hell anyway, so he was staying put. I explained to him that I had never seen anyone in that kind of hell in my readings. I told him he had already been through hell with Katrina and that he deserved to rest. I assured him he would be with his wife, who was waiting for him. I described her to him. At that point, and only then, did I feel an immediate rush of energy leave me. I almost collapsed because I felt so light.

However, I must admit that I often think of the souls of Katrina. I believe I helped them. I showed spirits love and compassion. I did not choose to gawk and stare or relish in their misery. I only wanted them to shift their vibration so they could live happier lives as spirits.

Sixteen years later while I was writing this book, New Orleans was once again struck by a devastating storm named Hurricane Ida on the exact same day (August 29th) as Hurricane Katrina. I cried and prayed for all the spirits of the city.

THE FLIP SIDE

Sometimes there are ghosts that you just do not want to deal with at all. They will latch onto you to drain you of your life force. They will plead with you not to let them go. These spirits can be very manipulative because they are indeed actually very desperate, and you may find yourself tempted to help them.

This was the case when I was younger. A young spirit found its way into my room. I am not sure if I brought the spirit home with me from somewhere or if it was attached to some item, but whatever the case, it was in my bedroom. It would often cry like a baby; although now I do not believe it was a child.

The more I tried to ignore this ghost the more it would throw tantrums. It would pull the covers on my bed and move things around in my room. I was accustomed to many of these antics from other spirits and even from my own energy, but this spirit grew angrier and angrier the more I tried to ignore it.

Of course, I knew nothing about different techniques to get rid of spirits except using my own rather strong energy. But I grew weary and finally capitulated to this ghost hitchhiking on my physical form. I probably carried this being around with me for over twenty years until a shamanic healer finally helped me release the ghost. I immediately had less depression and was healed of chronic migraines that I had experienced for years.

There are some energy beings that will drain you of your energy and make you ill. I know this without a doubt. Although I will communicate with different frequencies, I will never carry them around in this world. We are not meant to do that for energetic beings that have left their physical forms. Always be careful to not let one leech onto you!

Several of our healers and readers have sensed a very judgmental spirit being that lingers at SoulTopia. They have described him the same way, not even realizing that someone else gave the same description. The dude is much more menacing, primarily because he disapproves of what we do at SoulTopia. The ghost comes into SoulTopia from another nearby building.

He is tall and wears what looks like dark Pilgrim clothing. He will stand threateningly behind readers while they are working, and he will start down the hall where the healers' offices are located. Often, he will just materialize in front of me to startle me and scare others. I have often wondered if he is one of my ancestors who disapproves of my choice to open SoulTopia.

Everyone has energetically cleared him out of the store in the past, but I have instructed them that I want to talk to him. I want to explain my choices and communicate with this spirit. I feel confident he will not want to listen as he represents stubborn self-righteousness, but I will try. He is a ghost. But he is a spirit on a mission, and I am willing to talk to him at least to give him one opportunity to see my flip side.

Poltergeists

This type of spirit is perhaps the most feared by people because it allegedly has the most significant ability to affect our physical world. Poltergeists are believed to be responsible for unexplained noises, such as wall-banging, rapping, footsteps, and even music. They take our possessions or they may hide them. They may freak us out and return our possessions later. They turn on faucets, slam doors, turn lights on and off, and flush toilets. They want attention. The more attention they don't get, the more they throw a temper tantrum. They may throw things across rooms. They have been known to tug on people's clothing or hair. They have been said to slap and scratch the living. It is because of these some-times "mean-spirited" manifestations that some consider poltergeists to be demonic.

I have dealt with poltergeists since I was young. It has never been con-sistent, and I really cannot explain what triggers their occurrence. Most of the events when I was younger would occur in my bedroom or the powder room area I spoke of earlier. I recall one time when I was sent to my room, and all the art fell off the wall at one time. I was not allowed to hang anything on my walls, so it was not a lot, only what was there for decoration, but it made an impression. There were other times things would just fly around the room like a whirlwind.

I also had a cassette tape recorder I used. I would record myself talk-ing. I remember how I would often play it back, and there would be music playing or voices mumbling behind my voice that had not been there when I recorded it. As I've grown older, the occurrences are more about electronics. I tend to break all of them I am around, even if I do not touch them. Also, the television will still do the old-timey thing where it turns static even though televisions do not do that anymore. One inter-esting thing is that it will do it the minute my husband leaves the room and normalize when he returns to the room.

Sometimes I wonder if these poltergeist incidents are associated with my energy versus a poltergeist. I do have powerful energy. I was a kind, young girl, and I am a kind woman, but I have a strong temper that is energetically unruly if left unchecked. As it turns out, many people believe poltergeists are associated with teenage girls. I am not a teenager but that rebellious and restless energy remains within me.

INTRODUCING

Disincarnates are spirits who have left the body. In other words, they are what many call ghosts. Ghosts are typically defined as deceased humans still residing with individual consciousness for some unknown purpose. Their life force has left, but they have remained trapped here for some reason. The reason may initially be due to fear or desire to stay with a loved one, but in many cases, these disincarnates become restless over time.

IDENTIFYING

There are various forms of disincarnate energies.

Residual Imprints

Ghosts are distinguished from residual images in this chapter. A residual imprint is not a ghost per se. The energetic imprint of the memory or residual energy is strongly tied to the person, place, thing, or event. The imprint is more of an image or sound on a loop involving repeated actions. An example of a residual impression or imprint is a man on a battlefield who seems stuck in a repetitive loop repeatedly making the same motion. Residual imprints do not notice or interact with anything or anyone around them unless it is part of the repetitive loop. Residual imprints can occur in the form of any type of energy, including trains and elevators.

My husband, Roger, grew up in Mississippi where there are many old battlegrounds. He would often visit his grandmother's house and sit on her porch swing. He remembers seeing a soldier walk across the land attached to his grandmother's property. Even though he was young, he was not frightened by the ghost. The figure made the same motions repeatedly, and my husband now realizes it was probably a residual imprint of the soldier.

VISITING SPIRITS

These kinds of spirits are more common than many realize. They usually appear to people close to them shortly after the spirit's death. Many spirits watch their funerals, so they are very close for the days until that time, and there is a perfect chance you will receive some type of visitation. They are aware they have died, and they can interact with the living. They most often bring messages of comfort to their loved ones to say that they are well and happy and not to grieve for them. These spirits may appear briefly. They may not continue to emerge, and this often saddens loved ones. Please know that they do this for your good. They want you to experience your earthly journey to your fullest.

Contrary to moving on, they, of course, want you to remember them but not to cling to them solely. Loved ones are with you. They intentionally return with messages for the express purpose of helping the living cope with their loss.

Lorie has experienced several spirit visitations, and sadly, she is someone who has suffered significant loss. She was extremely close to her dad, Tim. He used to kid her about her numerous Christmas trees throughout her house. When he passed away, she became very depressed. That year she never took down her many Christmas trees. She eventually decided to turn one of them into a fall tree in her dad's honor. As she was decorating the tree with ornaments that he liked, such as fishing and hunting items, all lights in the house began to erratically flicker. There was no mistake that her dad was kidding with her in spirit.

However, the passing of her beloved dad was not the end of Lorie's dealings with loss. Her brother was at a party and went in the backyard to sit on a picnic table. No one else was around at that time, and sadly Johnny shot and killed himself. Johnny does not visit Lorie very often, but it is a dream of him pulling away from her when he does. It is as though he is crawling backward away from her down a tunnel. She knows this is a visitation dream because it profoundly affects her—causing great sadness.

If this were not enough, a year later, her twenty-year-old daughter, Cari Ann, was out with a group of people, and tragedy struck. At some point, the so-called friends dumped Cari Ann at the ER entrance, where she later passed away. Lorie's beautiful daughter, with the voice of an angel, had just been left to die. But Lorie knows that Cari Ann is still with her in spirit. Lorie receives frequent visitations from Cari Ann. When Lorie is lying in bed at night, Cari Ann will grab her by the thumb. Lorie will wake up immediately and feel the energy of her oldest daughter beside her. This brings Lorie great comfort.

A year after Cari Ann passed away, Lorie and her two other daughters went to their beach house in Florida. On the way, they decided to each pick a symbol to represent a sign from Cari Ann. Lorie picked a pink feather, one daughter picked a watermelon, and one picked an orange. When they arrived in town, they went to a restaurant, but it was so crowded they could not be seated and had to find another place to eat. At the next restaurant, right as they walked in, the owner had a plaque hanging on the wall of where his son had also passed away the year before. There was a remembrance book with a pink feather pen to sign the book. That led Lorie to open up about Cari Ann, and the man gave Lorie the pen to take with her. Later in their stay, they had a rainy day at the beach and ended up going to a store to get some games and puzzles. The moment the girls hit the game aisle, there were giant watermelon and orange squishy balls. The girls were ecstatic to know their sister was with them on their trip. Lorie still has the pink feather, watermelon ball, and orange ball. In addition, she frequently finds pink feathers.

Lorie believes that the spirits of her loved ones are with her. Perhaps that is what has helped her bear these losses in the physical realm with such dignity and grace. Lorie helps many others with a Facebook group called *A Little Honey in Heaven*. If you have lost a loved one, this group might help you connect with others who provide love and support.

Typical Ghosts

Ghosts are traditionally thought of as the spirits of the dead stuck between this realm and the one where they would cross or go after their spirit leaves their physical body. Many people will make a big fuss over the difference between a ghost and a spirit. They label the spirit as one who has crossed over and a ghost as one who has not. While these labels might help to avoid confusion, both are spirits in the sense that they are not in a physical body.

Most believe ghosts are caught or stuck here for a reason. The most common reason given is because of a tragedy or trauma of some sort. It is also thought that ghosts are often stuck here because they died under the influence of drugs, or they killed themselves. These are outmoded religious judgments, and I take significant issue with them. Perhaps the ghost was unhappy, which led to the addiction or suicide, but that does not make them low vibration beings.

It is high time we stop repeating such judgments. If they stick around, it may be to help people understand why they killed themselves. However, many ghosts choose to stick around to right injustices such as unsolved murders, improper burial, forced suicides, or negligent tragedies. They also may help correct ethical and moral failures such as stealing land from Native Americans and forcing people into slavery.

Ghosts also may stick around because they are not ready to leave, they fear judgment if they move to a different vibration, or they have someone here on Earth they feel a responsibility to help. Many believe these ghosts do not even realize they are dead, especially at first. These ghosts exist in a limbo state and may hang out where they died or in pleasant areas in life. Many, if not all, have an awareness of those living in their physical bodies. This distinguishes them from residual images. Some of these spirits can interact with those beings still in physical form.

Typically, ghosts will not appear in their healed form. However, spirits that cross to a different vibration than earth will often appear as whole or healed. Therefore, one way to identify a ghost is that they are not healed. They have not left the dense vibration of the earthly realm, and that is why many appear as they did when they died.

We have several ghosts at two of our SoulTopia locations. I used to not want to tell anyone about them because of some people's lack of understanding regarding ghosts. Allow me to explain before I tell you about our SoulTopia ghosts. Some people love to blame everyone and everything for their energy. Instead of checking their energy, they will proclaim a person, or a store has *negative* energy. We work very hard at SoulTopia to maintain uplifting vibes as opposed to funeral home vibes. Our music is fun, and the store is clean physically and energetically.

So that is why I was very protective when I realized we had visitors. Many of our readers and other workers have met our little girl ghost. She runs back and forth in the back of one of our stores. I often catch her out of the corner of my eye, and she will instantly make me laugh. She appears as a complete physical body apparition to me.

Tracey, one of my dear friends who leased an office at SoulTopia, had many encounters with the little girl. Tracey would be in the office late into the night when she was writing her romance novels. She would go into the kitchen to get water, and all the cabinet doors would be shut. She would sense the little girl's presence and see the girl in her mind's eye or third eye. Tracey would head back to her office and work a couple of hours, then realize she needed more water. On more than one occasion, Tracey headed back into the kitchen only to find all the cabinet doors open as well as all the drawers. Tracey indicated she never felt threatened or frightened; in fact, she was amused.

Those of us who encountered the little girl discussed if we needed to help her move along into a different phase of her beingness (some would call this helping her cross to the light). We all agreed that the spirit was happy with us, and that was where she needed to stay.

We all check in with her and communicate with her quite often to ensure she still is where she needs to be. We realize this is not, and will not be, permanent.

Practice
11 Things to Look for
Regarding Spirit Visitations

The following will help you notice when you have had a spirit visitation. Perhaps this list will help you accept it as a visitation instead of dismissing it as your imagination or a coincidence.

1. A Nonphysical Encounter

   You might not be able to see the spirit. A spirit may be in your presence, and you can just sense it. The energy in the room may just suddenly shift—you can't explain it—you just know it.

2. Touch

   A spirit may gently touch your hair or place its hand on your shoulder or hand. This will be a reassuring touch that carries the same emotion as a pat on the back or a hug.

3. Dreams

   Spirits will often visit you in dreams. The dream will feel very real.

4. Scent

   You may smell your grandmother's favorite perfume or your grandfather's cigars. Food and flowers are also popular aromas that you might smell, and you will recognize them as the person's favorite.

5. Hearing Their Voice

   You may hear them speaking to you and calling out your name. It may be an inner or outer hearing. It may sound just like them, or it may sound otherworldly, but you will know it is them.

6. Rearrangement of Items

   Items in your home that have some meaning to you might suddenly be rearranged with no explanation as to how they were moved.

7. Physical Appearance

   The spirit may appear to you in partial or total physical form. This might be a very hazy or misty figure or a full-bodied apparition. The person will appear healthy, unlike many ghosts.

8. Out of Body Visitation

   There are times you may enter a deep meditative state of sleep and you leave your body to meet with another spirit. This is about frequency adjustment and the fact that there is no veil dividing you.

9. Phone Calls

   Your phone may ring with the number of someone who has passed, and their phone has been disconnected. Another way spirits communicate through the phone is to bring up an old message long ago deleted to the top of your voice mails.

10. Items

    Anything in the physical world that the spirit can manipulate to get your attention is fair game. They may turn lights on and off, knock items off a shelf, or play their favorite song.

11. Symbols

    This is a prevalent way that spirits visit you. They remind you they are right there with you by sending you a simple sign that represents something meaningful. Common symbols include but are not limited to: birds, butterflies, feathers, flowers, rainbows, or anything you associate with happiness, contentment, and peace. You must observe the context and activity of the symbol to know what message the spirit is sending in the visitation.

CONNECTING

Ghosts are energetic beings, and they deserve compassion. They are not here for our amusement. One of my biggest pet peeves is a ghosthunter who—well, maybe just a ghosthunter. The word "hunt" has a negative connotation. Why would someone want to hunt a ghost? Why do they agitate spirits? This is disrespectful and uncompassionate. Ghosthunters are just capitalizing on the misery of another energy's suffering. This includes haunted hotels that use ghosts for marketing purposes. It is unethical. Yes, I realize that's a judgment.

Perhaps they should be spirit helpers. A spirit helper would possibly go to places thought to be haunted and get to know the spirit or spirits. They could help them move on to a different vibration, or *go to the light*, as many people call it.

That raises the question: Where do we usually encounter ghosts? It is generally accepted that ghosts are reported in hospitals, nursing homes, funeral homes, and cemeteries that are typically associated with the ghost's death. It is also generally accepted that ghosts are encountered in tragic natural disasters such as the Great Storm of 1900, a hurricane in Galveston, Texas in the United States. This was the deadliest natural disaster in United States history and the fifth deadliest Atlantic hurricane of all time.

Another common place to encounter ghosts is where tragedies or traumas occurred. However, what makes me raise an eyebrow is that the stories told always seem to be about old places or old times. This is highly questionable because, to be blunt, people die all the time, and there are many spirits in all types of locations.

There are many more spirits around us that you can connect with at any time if you begin to accept the concept of vibration being the only veil. However, if we stick to the typical idea of a ghost, they will usually make themselves known to us, or we will suspect they are around. If you can sense them around you, you may wonder (as I have for many years) why there are so many writings that just seem to repeat things you do not observe.

That is why I wrote this book. I read five books a week, and many repeat the same things over and over, and frankly, it feels like a bunch of bunk to me. It does not jive at all with what I see. There seems to be remnants of religious beliefs that do not hold true to me, such as those who die by suicide are stuck. No. That is not true any more than for someone else who dies. Why are those who die by suicide stuck? Because they failed their mission? I have never seen someone stuck as a punishment.

Some think you can't sense ghosts or cannot use any type of intuitive knowingness. I guarantee you can if you decide you want to do so. You do not need a bunch of equipment to interact with ghosts. Just start to sense shifts in energy. For example, there is a well-known hotel in California that is one of my favorite hotels. I did not even know ghosts inhabited it. I stayed there many times when my oldest son lived in Los Angeles. There was a basement part of the hotel that used to be a speakeasy. It is closed now due to health or zoning codes. I walked into one part of the speakeasy, and it felt pretty much standard.

I didn't think much, except it was really cool with old movie star photos on the wall. Then I walked a little further into the speakeasy, and the minute I crossed a specific area, the vibration shifted. I felt dizzy and as though I had crossed into a different dimension. Come to find out I had.

That area was the original speakeasy and it was known to be haunted. The first area had been added on at some later point. So, I thought, *Well, I've always been psychic. The next time we come, I will get someone else to walk across this area and find out if they feel a vibrational shift.* With no knowledge of anything, I snuck my husband Roger down to the basement and had him walk across the area. He immediately said he was dizzy, and it freaked him out, and he wanted to get out of there as fast as possible. Well, he can sense energy shifts because we all can. We might not all have the same experiences, but we can sense the shifts.

Practice
11 Ways to Know a Ghost is Near

The following will give you some tips to know when a ghost is around you. It is much more common than you might think. I do not use electronic gadgets because they are annoying and unnecessary to me, but some people, like my husband and other paranormal investigators, enjoy the use of equipment. You can use this list to practice becoming aware of all the spirits that are around you.

1. You hear soft voices when no one is there.
2. Your pets act strangely.
3. You feel a static electric charge in the air.
4. You see shadows or movements out of the corner of your eyes.
5. You feel like someone is watching you.
6. You feel like someone is touching you.
7. Some aromas cannot be explained.
8. You feel a shift in the energy in a particular area of a location.
9. You feel an overwhelming emotion in a specific place.
10. You are startled awake between 3:00 am to 3:30 am.
11. Things have been moved or misplaced.

Bonus: Just assume they are around, and do not be surprised to meet them!

PROTECTING

I encourage healthy dialogue with ghosts. They should only be avoided if they want to latch onto us. If they glom onto us, it will decrease our energy and even make us sick. Some of them may have a purpose of working in what might be called lower vibrational states. Perhaps they are meant to stay behind for a time to give us a message.

Why do we always dismiss them instead of asking them what they want from us? Most ghosts are not malevolent, contrary to popular belief. Fear is a powerful thing—especially the fear of the unknown. Perhaps the biggest unknown of all for most people is death. Therefore, most people are fearful of the spirits of the dead. However, more than anything else, most ghosts are harmless or even sad. If everything happens for a reason and you encounter a ghost, isn't there a purpose for that encounter? Why not attempt to discover what it is.

Of course, you should be prepared for the rare instance that the ghost might mean harm or might be a more evil type of spirit. Just as with any energy, there is duality, and there is a choice. So, of course, there are both ends of the spectrum and everything in between.

If you know you will be in a situation where you might encounter a ghost, you can protect yourself with a bracelet made of tiger's eye, hematite, and lapis. You can also carry sage if you want to ward off the spirit, but I would recommend not clearing the area until you are sure you want to remove the spirit. You might want to communicate with the spirit first. It may have a message for you. It may be a loved one.

I take a different approach and do not clear everything out automatically. I would want the opportunity to be heard, so I offer the spirits the same courtesy. Remember to "engage before you sage."

COLLABORATING

There are many reasons to collaborate with ghosts, but most involve receiving a message from them of how they can help us or how we can help them help someone else. If a loved one visits to provide us with a message to carry out on their behalf, we would probably want to do it if we loved that person.

But what about the visits that startle you? What if you walk into your room and an apparition or more full-bodied ghost is there? What if a spirit keeps opening and closing all the drawers to your nightstand?

What if they pull toys out of the toy box? The simple answer is to talk to them about why they are trying to get your attention.

These types of ghosts, which are around us much more than ghost-hunters ever report, used to scare me when I was little. They were always in my bedroom and I had trouble sleeping. I wanted to sleep with the lights on, but I was not allowed to do so. As I grew to communicate with spirits, ghosts stopped scaring me. They may startle me from time to time, but they do not scare me. That is because I know they want something. I just begin asking them what they want. I know they typically have a purpose. They don't slam windows just for the hell of it. They want your attention. Just give it to them. Simply tell them hello and ask if there is something you can do to help them.

You do not have to be a psychic medium to communicate with them. Just watch for signs. Listen to your inner knowing. Mediums are no different than anyone else who talks to an energetic being. Remember, it is just about the vibration and learning how to tap into that different vibration. The medium is a go-between. Suppose you want a medium, great. But you do not need one. They talk to those who have passed, but here we have learned that we are all energetic beings only divided by vibration. People love to make this much more complicated than it is.

HONORING

Instead of making sport of disincarnates, we should show them respect and dignity. One thing that upsets me is the way certain tourist spots and so-called ghosthunters treat ghosts. We should never attempt to agitate or disturb ghosts for sport. It is unkind. We should honor them. They were once someone's loved ones, even if they are not yours. They just want help with something.

DEMYSTIFYING

I am sure there are some decent ghosthunters. I know some paranormal experts that I greatly respect. But the ones who always act so shocked to encounter ghosts clearly have not seen many spirits because they seem so surprised when they claim they are in the presence of one. Spirits are everywhere. I do not know how to emphasize this enough. I am saying this as tactfully as I can—it is very difficult for me to take seriously a ghosthunter who is surprised to encounter spirits.

It is also important to remember that not all disincarnates are low energy. Yes, they have a different vibration that makes it challenging to move around at times, but that does not mean they are evil. Perhaps the evil is in agitating spirits. It is also important to realize that disincarnates can be encountered anywhere and at any time of year, month, or day. They are not limited to old, creepy places. They are all around us, and they walk among us.

8
The Spirit of a Land, Place, or Thing

There will often be the story of a ghost that becomes more about the land or the place. Such is the case with the Goatman's Bridge in Denton, Texas, United States. This area has a spirit all its own due to the collective consciousness of fear and sadness surrounding the bridge and the area. If you ever visit, you will feel the pestilent spirit immediately, even on a beautiful spring Texas day.

Denton County was formed in 1846. Around 1848, because of water shortages in other areas, the county seat was formed in a place they named Alton. However, the county seat was moved two more times and ended up in Denton. Today all that remains of the Alton village is the Baptist Church and the cemetery.

The Old Alton Bridge was built in 1884 to carry horses and later automobiles across the river. About half a century later, the bridge earned the name Goatman's Bridge because of an African American man named Oscar Washburn who had settled in the area. He made a living raising and selling goats and he posted a sign on the bridge that said *this way to the Goatman's*.

He was successful and well-liked by most with the exception of one group—the local Ku Klux Klan. His success angered them, and on a horrible night in 1938, they hanged Washburn from the bridge. However, when they looked to see if he was dead, his body had disappeared. The horrible tale says that the men were so angry they slaughtered Washburn's entire family.

There are all sorts of varying stories of the hauntings around the bridge. Ghosthunters have said it is the scariest place they have ever investigated. Here is what I know as a psychic medium married to a paranormal investigator: I become extremely sad when I visit. The last time my husband took a group there, I refused to go. The spirit of the place is not scary to me; although I am sure it is to others. To me, it is just extremely sad.

The bridge itself has a spirit all its own. The minute I step out of my car near the bridge, I can feel the bridge's vibration—it has just absorbed too much sadness and fear. The land around it was Native American land upon which people were slaughtered. The first time I visited the area, I actually *heard* the bridge—*this land is not your land, it is not my land, this land cries.*

Places, lands, and things can all have spirits associated with them or be spirits in and of themselves. They are energy. Since everything has energy, everything can hold energy. It is as though a house, a Native American burial ground, or a car can have a life of their own. They certainly can have the energy of a spirit. Do they have a soul? As I said in the introduction, I will leave it to you to draw your conclusions between spirit and soul.

As a child, I could never sleep. I think this is why I read so much; I would always take a book to bed with a flashlight if possible. I was always scared of what I would see or what would come into my room. My parents tried many things to help me sleep, including getting me a life-size Raggedy Ann doll, a life-size teddy bear, a ventriloquist's doll, and a clown. You read that right. These horror story items were sincerely intended to help me feel comforted. This did not work—no surprise there—especially the life-size Raggedy Ann doll. She would sit in a little antique rocking chair, and it did not take long for the doll to begin to have an energetic spirit.

While the teddy bear seemed to watch over me, the doll did not. The doll scared me, yet I felt like I had to pretend to like her. Her large button eyes followed me around my bedroom. I would try turning the doll the other way, but she somehow always seemed to settle back into her original position. Sometimes I would even put the doll in the closet. Let's just say that the doll's spirit did not like the closet any more than I did.

I recently regained custody of the doll. This is the same type of doll as the famous Annabelle doll even though the movie used a different-looking doll. I find it interesting that movies use a porcelain doll because of copyright issues and because they thought the Raggedy Ann doll was not as menacing. That is where they made a mistake, at least with me, because I was not moved or scared in the slightest in the movie or its sequels. After all, the scariest spirits are sometimes the ones that look the most innocent.

I do not believe in coincidences. I don't know how many of the Raggedy Ann dolls were manufactured, but the back story is there—something attached to at least my doll and the one on which the movie was based. The Annabelle doll is encased in a glass box in the museum of paranormal investigators Ed and Lorraine Warren. Gifted psychics will not even be in the same room with the doll. One thing is certain—it does not think it's a thing. It is a spirit in its own right.

THE FLIP SIDE

Many areas of land feel holy and soothing to the spirit. This concept is not new. In ancient Rome, the existence of *genius loci* (protective spirits) associated with specific locations. Sedona, Arizona is one such location. You can feel the uplifting power of the vortexes along with the majestic red rocks and beautiful greenery.

Glastonbury in England is said to be the burial place of King Arthur. Pagans and Christians mingle there and it is the heart chakra of Mother Earth.

Objects or things carry history. The history begins before we take custody of them. I was given a stool that had a beautiful embroidery by my grandmother. The love and care that went into finding the stool at a flea market, refinishing it, and then embroidering the beautiful cushion top remains in the stool. It has taken on not only the energy of my grandmother, but also a loving energy of its own. It represents something accomplished through pride and care rather than just haphazardly thrown together. People that don't even know the energy of the stool can feel its energy very easily.

IDENTIFYING

The idea of a land or place having its own spirit is not new. The idea is perhaps derived from the widespread belief that particular parts of the world are inhabited by spirits. *Genius loci* is Latin for the spirit or guardian of a place. In ancient times, the places were often sacred and associated with deities. This concept is broader in that the place may not just have a spirit associated with it but actually may be a spirit in and of itself.

These types of places, lands, or areas are identified by the intense energy surrounding the locality.

As with any spirit, this particular spirit may feel positive or negative. It may be a very sacred and holy place, or it may be a place of great tragedy. The point is that the spirit feeling is so strong that the masses are drawn to it or repelled by it. It doesn't take an extraordinary psychic to feel that this land or place has a life of its own.

Identifying a tangible item or thing that is a spirit is not always as easy. This might take someone who can sense the strong energy emanating from the spirit. However, some tangible spirits will make themselves known to most anyone. The issue is that most people think they are too educated to believe in such a thing. Well, the thing knows it is a spirit, and it is watching you whether you believe it or not. You see, your belief does create your reality, but there are also the thoughts of all the other energies surrounding you. They create reality also. So, open your eyes to the possibility of seeing the world of spirits right here with you.

Practice
11 Ways to Identify the
Spirit of the Land, Place, or Thing

The following practice will help you discern what you are dealing with regarding land, places, and things. It is important to know if the land, place, or thing is its own spirit being or if it has one attached to it.

1. Tap into the vibrational frequency of the land by researching or channeling the energy
   When dealing with the land, such as property or any area of land, you first must determine if you are dealing with a land spirit (land that has formed an energy identity of its own), spirit(s) residing on the land, or both. To do this, you need to know the history of the land.

2. Tap into the vibrational frequency of a place by researching or channeling the energy.
   When dealing with a place such as a house, you first must determine if you are dealing with a place spirit (a place that has formed an energy identity of its own), spirit(s) residing in or at the place, or both. To do this, you need to know the history of the place.

3. Tap into the vibrational frequency of a thing by researching or channeling the energy.

   When dealing with a thing such as doll, you first must determine if you are dealing with a thing spirit (a thing that has formed an energy identity of its own), spirit(s) residing in the thing, or both. To do this, you need to know the history of the thing.

4. Ask the spirit questions.

   Talk to the land, place, or thing. You may feel like you are talking to yourself, but you are not. Everything has energy—just begin to speak to that energy. Make sure to listen for the answers.

5. Use dowsing rods.

   Dowsing rods are forked twigs or L-shaped copper rods historically used to find water, ley lines, minerals, metals, and gravesites. These are useful for finding energetic hot spots on lands or at places. You set an intention for what you are searching for and then hold the rods and move about the property. The rods will cross as you get close to something of interest.

6. Use a pendulum.

   A pendulum is a small weight on a string or chain. Calibrate the pendulum for your use by asking it to show you a yes and no answer. The pendulum will move in a particular direction, and you will know this is your yes or no. It may require a little practice, but it is effective for answers and shows you directions. This may be useful for questions regarding things. Contrary to what many will tell you, a pendulum will not open a portal. You are the portal. That is a silly one that always really gets me. We are all portals.

7. Use clairtangency or psychometry.

   Physically touch the land, place, or thing to sense the energy.

8. Stay at the location. By staying on the land or at the place, you will see and feel what occurs while you are there. This will potentially be firsthand information instead of secondhand information.

9. Connect with the elementals.

10. Connect with the animals.

11. Ask your guides.

CONNECTING

To connect to a spirit place, simply go to the place. Before you get to the land or place, check in with how you feel physically, mentally, emotionally, and spiritually. Get to know your energetic frequency before stepping near the land or place.

Once you begin to approach the area, see if you notice any shifts in the vibrational frequency. Breathe in the energy. See if you like how it feels. You have experienced this at one time or another, perhaps without realizing it. Think of a building in your town that has had store after store go out of business. If you think back, you might recognize a funny feeling about the building. I am not referring to it being in a difficult location or having bad parking. I am talking about something about the building or area that just did not feel right. Perhaps you have walked into a field, and all of a sudden you felt a heaviness only to learn the land had a history of a massacre.

If you find a land or place that you feel has a spirit, please do not immediately assume that the spirit needs to be cleared. Who are you to jump to that conclusion? I implore you to first get in touch with the spirit. Is it the spirit of the land/place, or is it a spirit associated with it? Then follow the steps described in this chapter to determine what you want to do next.

If you have legal access and choose to continue connecting with the spirit, a great way to do so is simply by caring for it and getting to know it. If it is an area of land, you can keep it free of trash. Crystals such as green agate, green moss agate, and tree moss agate are ideal for placing around an area of land.

If it is a house, you can talk to the house. Touch the walls and try to connect with the energy. If it is empty and you are safe to enter, you can care for the home or the lawn. Black tourmaline and pyrite are ideal for placing around the home's perimeter to keep intruders away from the home.

Practice
11 Signs of the Use of Clairtangency (Psychometry)

The following will help you determine if you use clairtangency (clear touch, which is also known as psychometry) to intuitively gather information. You will know it when you read it! No scoring is necessary. You can use this list to practice your clairtangency.

1. Used clothing and jewelry don't feel right to you (clothes hold lots of energy).
2. Used furniture or antiques feel strange to you but you don't know why.
3. Pawnshops bother you (desperate energy).
4. You get vibes from restaurants or stores.
5. Cluttered spaces make you feel uncomfortable (scattered energy).
6. Messy house or workplace affects your mood (scattered energy).
7. You feel compelled to wash your hands after looking through used goods.
8. You feel compelled to wash your hands after touching crystals or rocks.
9. You tend to touch things to get a sense of them.
10. If you hold an item, flashes of information will come to you.
11. A building will almost speak to you if you touch its walls.

PROTECTING

If you have any questions about whether the spirit is benevolent or malevolent, you should always use protection. Nuummite and obsidian are probably the best crystals for something you think might be menacing. However, if you are sure of a spirit at a vibration that is not healthy for you, the best thing to do is just to stay away from that place or thing. But again, do not presumptively rush in to clear a spirit until much more information is gathered. One way to think of it is that we would not want someone to come and clear us or sage us away, plus unless someone knows how to transmute (change) the energy to a different form, they probably are not effectively clearing anything.

COLLABORATING

Spirit places/lands are lovely to collaborate with, especially when they are connected to nature. There is nothing more healing than the healthy vibration of beautiful land. You can also collaborate with a place or land to help it heal. Compassion for the place or land may lead you to want to team up with this spirit to help it become whole or have a new story to tell. The flip side of this is that some places, lands, or things carry a lot of sadness and anger. Please let me be clear—do not mess around with the spirits of places, lands, or things if you feel sad or angry.

Even living in a particular home can cause severe depression or even arguments among its residents. So, while I always advocate initially giving the spirit the benefit of the doubt, please know I have stared down death because of these very issues and lacked the proper tools to understand how to deal with all the spirits around me.

HONORING

Perhaps one of the most beautiful things you can do for any type of spirit is to honor the spirit of a place or land where many souls were lost, such as Native American lands. You should never do this without asking the landowner and the associated tribe the proper type of way to show honor. Donating money or even helping fight for the rights of the land might even be suggested.

You can honor and appreciate tangible items also. You can put them in an area where they feel comfortable instead of sticking them away in a box. My Annabelle doll is now in our guest bedroom in her rocking chair. I am in the process of getting all her friends out of boxes so they can join her.

The list of how to honor an item or thing is endless based on what it is, but giving it a position of prominence in your home is a simple way to start.

DEMYSTIFYING

The so-called negative side of land, place, or thing spirits could easily bleed over into what many refer to as possession. Just because somewhere or something has a spirit does not mean it is possessed. It is energy. It has just shifted in vibration. How you ultimately decide to think of this and label it is up to you. However, as mentioned before, I get pretty irritated when people jump to the conclusion that *all* spirits must be cleared from lands, places, and things. That conclusion presumes an authority over the spirit. I do not believe it is wise to assume that hierarchy because we are in a denser form of energy.

The other energy may have much more of a right to that land. Perhaps the land belonged to them long before you came along. Haven't many of us made those mistakes before? Presuming we have authority over someone else? I propose it is no different if the energy is in spirit form.

9
Thought Forms, Demons, and Predatory Spirits

As mentioned earlier, not many things scare me at all these days in the way of spirits. While movies used to scare me, now I irritate people by laughing at how silly most of them are or by falling asleep during the movie. However, I know to respect the duality of spirits. If there are benevolent spirits, that same spirit or another one may choose to be equally malevolent. Some are genuinely insidiously so.

I met one such predatory spirit not too long ago. I was working in my bedroom while Roger, my husband, was sleeping. I had a light on my work and was fully awake. The rest of the room was dark. Roger was sound asleep. He had been struggling greatly with his diabetes and had lost a lot of weight recently. Earlier in the evening, he had told me his A1C (a test that measures blood sugar levels) was at 12. Imagine a thermometer with 13 at the top in the red danger zone. The 12 meant Roger's blood sugar had been very high for at least three months. With that concern in mind, I had been glancing at him from time to time as he slept.

Suddenly, there was a rotten smell in our room. It did not smell like sulfur (I say that because many people claim you will smell sulfur when ghosts are around). It just smelled like an old, rotten compost pile of decaying flesh. I quickly looked up at Roger and saw leaning over the area of his spleen, a short, older woman shrouded in dark black clothes and a veil. I leapt up and tried to keep my voice calm, but I was angry. What do you want? I asked. She just made a scoffing type of noise. I flew across the room faster than a spirit, and said, *I banish you from this room.* She laughed and was out of the room in an instant.

Well, if you think I was not scared, you are wrong because that is one of the scariest spirits I have ever encountered. If you haven't figured it out, meeting spirits is not a big deal to me. I expect them. Well, I made a big mistake this time. Did you catch it? I banished her from the room. We have three levels to our home, and it took me about a week to finally feel she was gone, not just from our bedroom but from our entire house. Roger got better. I am convinced she would have killed him that night.

THE FLIP SIDE

Carlton is one of the kindest souls I know. He also has a vast knowledge of ceremonial magick that has evolved into theurgy. He has come to realize he needs to be careful with the spirits he can create.

Carlton was ruthlessly bullied throughout his school days. We hear about kids being bullied a lot, but we really should pay more attention because those feelings go somewhere. Carlton is highly gifted in his psychic abilities, and this giftedness grew as he stuffed more and more feelings into food and alchemy. The more Carlton was bullied, the more he gained weight, and the angrier he became. To add insult to injury, Carlton's torturer was a straight, handsome male for whom Carlton had developed feelings. These feelings were unrequited, and Carlton became hurt and envious. Even though the male continued to physically and emotionally bully Carlton, Carlton's envy grew and grew.

Carlton claims his greatest sin was envy. So, Carlton created a golem to carry his worst sin. This golem was given consciousness and embodied the demon of envy—Leviathan. Eventually, however, Carlton's jealousy began to hurt others through the demon. The person who bullied Carlton ended up in the hospital badly injured. Carlton also ended up suffering extreme illnesses.

Carlton knew it was time to take hold of the situation, but he admits he didn't know the proper way to handle it at the time. He shoved the demon inside his consciousness, which led to self-medication and addiction. Years passed, and at the young age of twenty-seven, he found himself in a mental hospital. After a long battle of recovery, education, therapy, and renewed understanding, he emerged with his bachelor's degree and a new lease on life.

However, he still works with the golem. You see, Carlton holds himself accountable for the envy, not Leviathan. He explains the golem now as a firm hand on Carlton's shoulder, reminding Carlton that the demon will handle things. It lets him know when someone is being shady or makes presumptions regarding his motives, but now he healthily handles the information. Carlton does not have to succumb to his envy.

He has also learned that it is more about the karmic consequences others make, and he has learned to recognize this in himself. His golem helps him make better choices, especially in what he perceives as magick and the responsibility of using it.

INTRODUCING

Thoughts create reality. So obviously, thoughts are mighty forces. When you layer thoughts with emotion, you have the potential for energetic dynamite. Then when you begin to sustain your thoughts with a clear focus, the thoughts will start to take on a life of their own. Once you begin to feed the thought and repeat it in pattern-like form, a thought form emerges.

If others in a group sustain thoughts over time, it becomes a thought form of the collective consciousness. All these thought forms, like everything, are energy. These energetic thought forms are living spirits that are manifested by thoughts. These thought forms can be uplifting, or they can be life draining. Some intuitives can see thought forms while other people cannot, but everyone can create them. Some people may make them without even realizing it. A thought form is an entity and is no different than any other type of spirit.

Thought forms may be referred to as a tulpa. A tulpa has no consciousness because it is your emotion, and it has free will based on the servitor (the one it serves). The tulpa will do things based on your emotions and thoughts—and god knows what they will do. A golem is not a thought form. It is created out of mud and water, then given consciousness, and is tempered by the emotions of the servitor.

The word demon is derived from the Greek word daimon, meaning replete with wisdom. Demons are often referred to as spiritual beings of an angelic nature, often said to look for a body to possess or inhabit. They are considered interfering and self-propagating spirits. But many forget that if angels have free will, so do demons. In pre-Christian and non-Christian cultures, demons were not, and are not, always considered evil. However, by the sixteenth and seventeenth centuries, demonologists had created a hierarchy of demons corresponding to the hierarchy of saints and archangels so that the proper saint could be called upon to drive out a demon. The seven deadly sins were often thought of as demons—Lucifer-Pride, Belphegor-Sloth, Mammon-Greed, Beelzebub-Gluttony, Satan-Wrath, Leviathan-Envy, Asmodeus-Lust.

Predatory spirits are more insidious than a run-of-the-mill demon. A predatory spirit has come with a purpose. The purpose is usually to harm the one it appears to, or in many cases, a loved one of the ones for whom it appears.

In my experience, they only mean harm. However, I understand the duality of energy and assume these energies, which I have only ever seen and experienced as nasty parasites, do have, in some scenarios, the ability to have the free will to change.

IDENTIFYING

Have you ever considered that your thoughts are beings or entities? They are called thought forms or thought entities, but people have made them complicated. I invite you to just think of them more simplistically. Everything has energy—our thoughts have energy—thoughts are things. They may be fleeting or have many feelings (also part of beingness) that make them last longer and grow stronger. A thought form may be well conceived or a vague notion. Like any other energy being, the thought form has duality—it may be fear based or love based. We might call it positive or negative for ease of discussion, but always remember, we refer to vibrations, not the judgment of the vibration.

Our thoughts have specific vibrations that interact with all other energy. If you are angry enough, you can create a so-called negative thought form. You may even feed that energy by talking about it to others, dwelling on it, lighting candles in anger, calling the person names, and so on.

The point is the thought form is growing into a beast that needs to be fed. That thought form is kept alive by the energy of thoughts given to it. It may even glom onto other negative thoughts and feelings and grow seemingly out of control. In this way, our thoughts most certainly are creating our reality. It may even begin to control our reality and potentially that of others.

The thought continues to vibrate and grow based on the energy it is provided. Most people are not even necessarily aware of the thought form they are creating. For instance, they just know that they are incredibly jealous, and all their energy is going into the situation or person involved. However, some do intentionally work with thought forms.

Thought forms are used in magic and the casting of spells. Thought forms, including personalities, structures, objects, and places, can be created magically. These entities may be created and summoned to perform specific tasks, such as carrying out spells. Just like many spirits, thought forms are invisible to most people but can be perceived clairvoyantly.

These thought forms produce a radiating vibration. The lifespan of a thought form depends on the nature and intensity of the thought. Most thought forms dissipate. Those imbued with sufficient energy, either through the sustained power of thought or ritual magic, may stick around longer. The more these thought forms are focused upon, the more they continue to grow. They begin to radiate outward and attract more vibrations that are in alignment with them, which often makes them proliferate. This is through the Law of Attraction, where like attracts like. Archetypes, mythological deities, a character in movies, or movies themselves can turn into thought forms.

An example of this is Harry Potter. The character and the movie took on a beingness and life of their own. Harry Potter was one character, and he brought everyone into his world. He did this by taking on a real world and magical world hero's journey. He showed us how we could have energy manifest in our own life.

Harry Potter became part of the collective consciousness and collective norm. If the collective consciousness puts sustained energy into these thought forms, they continue to form. When the interest wanes, the thought form will begin to dissipate. Groupthink can create a thought form. The stronger the energy, the stronger the thought form.

Thought forms can assume their energy and appear to be intelligent and independent. Equally, intense thought can disperse them, or they can simply disintegrate when their purpose is finished. Some may last moments, while some may last centuries. Always remember that there can be all different vibrations of thought forms. They are not all just negative.

The critical thing to remember with thought forms and demons is that you want to identify them. You want to become aware of what type of spirit you are dealing with at all times. Does this vibration fit what you want to accomplish? Is it lifting your energy or draining it?

It is straightforward to identify a predatory spirit. They are hunting something. They want something. They are condescending and snide. They do not care about your morals or religion. They are quickly cleared with vigilance, or when their prey is gone. However, they may carry a horrible stench. You will recognize them immediately, and you will be frightened because that is what they want and the vibration they have. They prey on the weak.

Practice
11 Steps to Create a Thought Form

The following practice will teach you how to create, use, and release a thought form.

1. Calm your thoughts by learning to control your breathing.
   To manage your breathing, slow down long enough to inhale to the count of three and exhale to the count of three. Bring your focus to your breath. Every time your thoughts wander away from your breath, bring your focus back to the three counts of inhaling and exhaling.

2. Calm your emotions by continuing to focus on your breathing.
   Thoughts and emotions are very closely intertwined. Your emotions are the fuel for the thought forms, so before creating one, you need to get your emotions in check.

3. Bring your attention to your thoughts.
   At this point, your thoughts should not be racing. They should be calm, and you can simply breathe into them.

4. Breathe into a focused thought.
   As you calmly bring your attention to your thoughts, you can direct the attention to one succinct feeling you want to home in on instead of your ideas being all over the place.

5. Decide on the purpose of the thought form.
   Now that you have your thoughts focused and your emotions in check, it should be pretty simple to decide the purpose. Perhaps you want the thought form to help you stand up to a bully. Maybe you want the thought form to keep you company through a difficult breakup. Whatever the purpose, try to be as detailed as possible

because you are creating reality with your thoughts. So, you want to be very specific.

6. Create the form and function of the thought form.

   It is usually easiest to base your thought form on something you are familiar with, such as an animal, mystical creature, or a human. This familiarity helps you be able to give form and function to your thought form more easily. You want the form and personality to fit the purpose. For instance, you might not envision a hamster standing up to a gang of bullies. Perhaps a lion would be better suited for the form and function of the purpose.

7. Associate the thought form in a vessel if desired.

   If it helps you visualize your thought form better, you can connect it to a statue or a photo. The thought form will be energetically one with the vessel.

8. Empower the thought form.

   The best way to do this is to let your emotions flow into the thought form. When your feelings regarding the situation become linked with your thoughts, you already have a thought form—you are just ramping up the energy now. You do want to be careful not to let the emotions get out of control.

9. Set parameters around your thoughts, i.e., your thought form.

   At this point, check your emotional frequency. How something sits with you ethically is your moral compass check. Make sure you are not letting anything manifest in this thought form that you will regret later. This is a creation from your thoughts, and you are responsible for setting parameters such as not breaking the law, following rules of karma, or doing no harm.

10. Give the thought form a task.

    If the thought form was created to protect you from bullies, you could tell it, "You are here to protect me from these bullies by making me invisible to them." If you need companionship during a time of a bad breakup, let the thought form know it is here to keep you company.

11. Reward and release the thought form.

Always treat thought forms with respect of an ene-rgy being. If your thought form helps you, reward it with your positive thoughts and gratitude. When the purpose is fulfilled, your thoughts will drift from the need for this thought form. Give gratitude as the energy fades away. When the purpose of the thought form has run its course, go through these steps and deconstruct the thought form in love.

CONNECTING

Thought forms are as easy to connect with as your thoughts. The sustaining of them is what may take some effort. If you intentionally create a thought form to do a task for you, then you will have to put a lot of your time and energy into thinking about that issue. Predatory spirits are also easy to connect with on one condition. They almost always want something and prey on someone they perceive as weak in mind, body, or spirit. Although they are as easy to connect with if weaknesses or vulnerabilities are present, they are suprisingly easier to get rid of unless they are on the hunt. In other words, they act tough, but if you just call their bluff and stare down those hideous losers, they will back off even more quickly than they connected. The only real problem is when someone wants to bargain with them or is too weak to stand up to them.

PROTECTING

Use protection when working with these spirits. I protect through the energy of my mind and intention. I believe it is the most potent protection we have. If you choose to work with these spirits, I suggest calling on the archangel counter to the demon.

Simply put, I do not cast circles. Well, I take that back. I do it all with the energy of my mind. I let my mind surround my beingness with solid protective light and a high frequency of love, and I let some high-energy beings step in and do the rest of the work. Archangel Michael is no wimp. He will protect you. But do not underestimate your ability to set firm boundaries of protection.

Although there may be a time when we may want to ask a predatory spirit what it wants, do not engage too much with these spirits as they are very skilled tricksters. There may be a time when you may want to ask what business predatory spirits have with you, and eventually, you want to banish these spirits from your home and life. They are relatively easy to get rid of because they will seek easier prey if you stand up to them. However, they are not spirits you want to ever toy around with because you will suffer consequences.

Nicole's first paranormal experience was when she was in the second grade. Her family lived in her mother's hometown of Woodstown, New Jersey. Nicole and her younger brothers shared a bedroom with Nicole in one bed and the boys in the other. There was a window between their beds and one that was on the wall the bed was pressed against (at the foot of their bed).

One night after they had gone to bed, Nicole remembers waking up and being compelled to look out the window. At the same time, her middle brother did the same. There was a man who looked like a vampire at the window. Nicole's first thought was *its the end of November, why would someone be wearing a vampire costume* (she was very logical even as a child).

The man started to talk to them. *Please invite me in. Please let me in.* He did this about three times. Nicole started to feel what she later realized was evil emanating from him. She pulled her head away from the window and he appeared to move toward the other window. Nicole's brother moved and Nicole thought he was going to go to the other window to let in the vampire. She started to scream, and their parents came running. When their dad checked outside no one was there and the heavy reel trashcan that was against their window had not been moved.

Nicole's father entered the Army not long after and they moved. It was always a memory she carried and eventually when they were adults, the siblings verified they had seen the same thing. It gave Nicole a lifelong fear of windows without shades, and looking back this was also her first of a life of paranormal experiences. They had various experiences in each place they lived but that one was probably one of the scariest.

A lot of people don't believe in evil. However, Nicole felt it from that creature that night. Not knowing for sure if it was a human spirit, a demon, or an actual vampire, she does know it was evil. There is no doubt in her mind. Throughout her life whenever she picks up something similar from a person, place, or situation—she knows to get out of there ASAP.

It did try to contact her again a few years ago. She was getting the feeling that it was time to move on from her job at the time but wanted a second opinion. She went to SoulTopia to a channeler who was a long-time friend of the store and incredibly talented. As a reader herself, she felt safe and knew she would get a good reading. As the reader started to channel, she has asked that only things that were for Nicole's highest and best good come through in the reading. She proceeded to bring up that a spirit guide wanted to work with Nicole to help her with her potential.

This type of reading was nothing new to Nicole and, although she trusted the reader, her spidey senses began creeping up—this felt like a familiar evil. In fact, the being was masking himself from this incredible reader, but not from Nicole! She knew what his essence felt like, and Nicole knew his frequency. Towards the end of the reading, the reader mentioned Dracula, which validated Nicole's knowingness. Nicole is not scared of spirits. In fact, she will work with shadow side spirits on many occasions, but Nicole also knows when to not mess around with a spirit that is taunting her.

Practice
11 Ways to Protect Against Psychic Attack

The following will give you ways to protect against a psychic attack from any type of spirit, including humans.

1. Most importantly, do not succumb to the power of suggestion. Do not assume every time you are tired that someone has put a curse on you. This is one of my biggest pet peeves—people falling for the fact that they have been cursed. While I believe in the power of strong malicious energy directed at someone (a curse), I do not think that everything that happens to us is a curse. Most people are too busy with their own lives to sit around hexing you. You are just feeding it more energy when you dwell on whether someone has put a curse on you. If you insist on believing you have a curse, get someone responsible to show you how to remove it. Do not pay them money to do so!

2. Be aware of your energy when going through any type of trauma or grief. Parasites look for this opportunity.

3. Avoid drugs and alcohol. Also, get an energetic clearing after any anesthesia because you are susceptible to attack when under anesthesia.

4. Avoid self-sabotaging thoughts or negative self-talk.

5. Be careful of frequencies of spirits that seem to talk down to you.

6. Take a break from the news and social media.

7. Challenge them in a lucid dream. Then you can kick their butts.

8. Simply cross your hands across your solar plexus or stomach area.

9. Ask your guides to step in and handle it.

10. Be careful of anyone putting you in a hypnotic state—in other words, make sure they are reputable.

11. Be confident in your powerful energy but not cocky.

COLLABORATING

Thought forms are ideal for collaboration if you can manage your energy and emotions the way you want the outcome to go. If not, you may be playing with fire, and you and others can and will get burned. I encourage you to take in every experience you can and bear witness to them. This ability to bear witness is so you can know what not to do. So, if you do or observe something not in your moral wheelhouse, you won't ever do it again. It comes down to being mature enough energetically to know what you can work with and what you cannot.

Many of you are called to work with some shadow side beings. Some of you have stared it down so that you can help others. Be careful of any spirit that has a price for their collaboration and know if you are willing to pay the fee. I have paid the price for many intentional and unintentional collaborations. The choice is up to you.

HONORING

I look at honoring these spirits more as respecting the seriousness of the energy. I have borne witness to many who toy with spirits they have no business flirting with, and those spirits have taken their pound of flesh. Some spirits just do not deserve any honor.

DEMYSTIFYING

Whatever you or anyone calls these spirits, they are as real as spirits of the light. The Law of Polarity and the Law of Duality are no joke. And since these spirits are real, they walk among us just as much as spirits of the light. Often, these spirits are self-propagating—we create them through the intense emotions we have. Emotions such as anger can get out of our control quickly.

Every culture has different beliefs and names for these lower vibrations. Still, they feel the same no matter what they are called and can provide you with beneficial information to channel. For those who become desperate to channel information, they can also be very tempting because they can give you what many people would call spot-on information as much as beings of the light can.

After serious contemplation, I can say I know I have walked with shadow spirits for a reason. I do not doubt that I allowed some into my life by acting out my self-loathing. Those low vibration spirits then propagated more low vibrations. However, some came into my life to teach me how to defend myself and help those in the depths of despair. Make no mistake! These spirits are as accurate as spirits that choose a vibration of light. Always remember the Law of Polarity. Some of these spirits are self-propagating predators, and they only appear to cause some sort of serious harm, or even death.

10
Multidimensional Beings (Extraterrestrials)

Have you ever met someone and thought they just do not seem Earthly? Have you ever felt that way about yourself? When I first met a client named Karla, I immediately thought *Well, you aren't from here*. I thought I had said it to myself but realized I had said it out loud. She smiled politely and mentioned that she had a lot to learn. Although she had an otherworldly appearance, I have learned not to base assumptions on that because I know how energy works and how spirits can change forms. Nonetheless, she looked part elf, part faery, part angel, and part alien of the Pleiadian or Lemurian type.

It took me only one or two sessions with Karla to discover she did not need me as any type of spiritual mentor at that time except to help her know how to tap into her true self. Karla is one of the kindest people I have met on Earth while also being firm in her boundaries. I know that she is on Earth to raise the collective vibration. I suggest you read this chapter with an open mind to all the world of spirits of every kind among us.

INTRODUCING

Multidimensional beings are just as they sound. They not only can travel between dimensions but have existed in multiple dimensions, either at different times or simultaneously, depending on your perspective and understanding of non-linear time. They lived on Earth in physical form in the distant past and possibly still do in the present. Many of us carry the DNA of multidimensionals and are utterly unaware of it. We have not yet discovered some of our abilities as a result. Other hybrids may be living among us who have shape-shifted into forms that allow them to blend in and interact with us more easily. For example, you, your child, or your postal worker could be a starseed.

A starseed is a spiritual being that did not originate on Earth but is from a distant galaxy, star system, planet, or possibly a different universe. These advanced intellectual beings volunteer to come to Earth for some reason. Starseeds typically do not feel like they belong on Earth, but they know they need to be here. They are drawn to the stars and most have a solid empathic nature.

Like any other spirit being, starseeds can choose benevolence, malevolence, or any other label on the spectrum of beingness. Most have had some trauma in their lives. As mentioned earlier, many of those who easily see and sense spirits have had a traumatic event either physically, mentally, or emotionally. I believe we are all starseeds. It is just a matter of figuring out which one or combination of them you are. Unlocking the combination is accomplished in the same way you would connect— through frequency compatibility.

Originally, the multidimensionals came to Earth from other star systems within our physical plane, but they have also inhabited other planes of existence in different dimensions and realms. (See appendix for more in-depth information about planes, dimensions, and realms.)

Multidimensionals from these other planes of existence, dimensions, and realms visit our physical plane, but in the form of spirits, not as physical beings (like the hybrid shape-shifters). Like any other being we characterize as a spirit, they are not hidden behind any kind of veil. We just have to adjust to their frequency to detect and communicate with them.

In the context of this book, we will cover some of the multidimensionals that are walking among us in spirit and physical form.

IDENTIFYING

The same names come up over and over again: Atlantis, Pleiades, Orion, Lemuria, and more. If they truly existed, then where were they? Scholars have debated this and have reached no consensus. Atlantis could have been anywhere from Bimini, Santorini, Easter Island, Vanuatu, or the Caribbean. The best bet is that all these locations were part of the vast Atlantean empire.

Were they lost and gone forever? No! Perhaps physical evidence will never be found, but the energetic imprint still exists, and it's possible that the *physical proof* does also. We simply cannot see it. It comes down again to a matter of frequency.

The Atlanteans, who were cerebral beings and very technology oriented, could very likely have had the ability to hide Atlantis using dark matter that does not radiate electromagnetic light. But since the location of these civilizations considered lost is not the focus of this book, let's instead discuss some of the multidimensional spirits we may encounter.

While some physical attributes are given, please know that because most of these spirit beings can shape shift, it is once again my opinion to go much more on characteristics regarding frequencies rather than physical appearances.

Lyran Starseed

Lyrans, with their feline-like features, initially come from Vega, the brightest planet in the Lyra constellation, which is 32,900 light-years away. When you think about Lyrans in the galaxy, you can compare them to Romans or Egyptians on Earth—ancient or first civilizations. As such, they are Earth's ancestors.

The peaceful Lyrans, having never known war or deception and lacking a defense system, had to flee their homeland when the invading Draconians wiped them out by the billions. Facing extinction, they broke into three distinct factions and left for other worlds.

These starseeds are the oldest souls, having lived many lifetimes on other planets and galaxies before coming to Earth. They help us realize our true nature and the value of a strong work ethic. They also gave us fire.

Although they are very grounded, analytical, and hard workers, Lyrans are fiercely independent, enjoy freedom, love travel, and enjoy life to the fullest. They are athletic, fearless, and adventurous. They are assertive and will defend themselves and others against injustice. Due to their ancient wisdom, they understand the transient nature of our physical beingness.

Andromedan Starseed

Andromedan starseeds are very rare. They find it the most difficult to adjust to Earth because of the difference in frequencies. They originated only 2.5 million light-years away from Earth from a spiral galaxy known as the Andromeda Galaxy, sometimes called Messier 31 or M31. It was also home to the Pleiadians, Lyrans, and Sirians.

They have appearances much like ours but are also seen as tall with wings, leading many to believe they are angels. The Andromedans are of a much higher vibration, and Earth feels very heavy to them. However, they can help us open up to these higher frequencies and connect with them. These old souls are connected to the Akashic Records—the records of all that is, was, and ever will be.

These high vibrational beings feel uncertain on Earth because of the frequency difference, but this doubt is not warranted. You see, one thing they understand that many of us and many of our teachers have failed to realize is that we can ascend right here on Earth! Let me repeat that— you do not have to leave Earth to ascend.

Andromedans understand that. They understand how to astral travel and connect to higher dimensions. They value their freedom and love change and adventure. They tend to have no sense of Earth time and are therefore rarely punctual.

They lead simple, low-key, humble, and private lives. They are drawn to teach others primarily to help them expand and awaken to the higher consciousness that can exist in us all.

Sirian Starseed

Sirians originate from the planets Sirius A and Sirius B, both located within the Canis Major (Dog Star or Star of Isis) constellation. The likes of Jesus and Mother Mary came from the brightest star in Earth's sky— Sirius A. Its original inhabitants came from Vega, in the Lyra constellation, the supposed home of Earth's ancestors. Merpeople and all other water beings came from Sirius B. Sirius A and B started the awakening of Earth beings. They are also said to have interacted with the Egyptians to build the pyramids. Greek god Anubis is said to have been a Sirian.

Sirian starseeds find it hard to communicate verbally because they are used to communicating telepathically just like the Lemurians. Sirians are animal and nature lovers including the multidimensional animals such as unicorns and Sasquatch. They are very driven and determined at whatever they set out to do. They pick their friends carefully and have a tight inner circle, but they are loyal to the end once they are your friend. They get bored quickly and want to stay busy because they are doers. They are pretty connected to Earth's frequency and just settle in and get things done. They rarely get angry and help keep the peace.

Pleiadian Starseed

Pleiadians are highly evolved and loving spirits that come from a star cluster known as the Pleiades (also known as Seven Sisters, Messier 45, and the Eye of the Bull) within the Taurus constellation. They behave a lot like humans but are much more spiritually and emotionally evolved. They are here among us to help uplift and heal us. Often, they will have talents they are not even aware of until they stumble upon them.

They are loving, nurturing, sensitive, and creative beings here to help heal our souls. We might call them empaths. While here, many of them will be involved in any activity that brings healing or balance, such as medicine, social justice, or the law.

They know they are here for a purpose, but they may not know precisely what it is, and that is perfectly ok. You see, they understand a crucial concept—purpose is not necessarily about something specific. It may simply be about bringing joy and laughter to those around you.

They work closely with the Arcturians, which you will read about later in this chapter.

Lemurian Starseed

I think of Lemurians as the hippies of the starseeds. Not wannabe kind of hippies, but the ones that truly believe in equality for all. Lemurians are gentle, innocent, and perhaps a bit naïve. They were so good that it probably led to their destruction eons ago. They simply believe that everyone is pure and loving like them. At one time they had a utopian society. They did not adhere to any hierarchal structures. If you were a high priestess in the temple or a farmer in the garden, you were equal.

This feeling of equality is one sure-fire way to identify someone who claims to be a Lemurian on Earth today. If someone is bragging about being a Lemurian or acting superior, they are probably not Lemurian. Lemurians lived in close-knit communities, not only with their own family but other families. They were also freer in their definition of parameters on relationships. There was much love for the community as a whole because Lemurians have a strong belief in the oneness of all beings.

Physically, Lemurians are typically in shape, or are not happy that they have let themselves get out of shape. However, they may pad with weight for protection from specific energies. They often have long hair and perhaps have tattoos. They are hardworking, but also know how to relax and enjoy themselves. They are accessible in spirit and relationships. They love the outdoors because they are very connected and protective of Mother Earth. Therefore, many are animal advocates and environmentalists. They are fluid in relationships and open to trying different forms of sexuality.

Lemurian spirits face some challenges. If they are unawakened, they may turn to substance abuse to escape what they consider to be a harsh world. This tendency toward addiction might cause them to linger once they have passed. They are also much like untrained empaths in that they tend to see good in all, so sometimes they put everyone else's needs before their own. This need to care for others also may cause them to feel the need to stick around a loved one once they pass to watch over them.

Their strengths are bringing groups together, teaching, spreading tolerance, shamanic work, and working for the good of all. They are laid-back, creative thinkers who are loyal and trustworthy. Just like empaths, Lemurians may want to hide away from the mainstream; however, if they will stop hiding they can bring about significant changes to a hurting world.

Atlantean Starseed

Atlanteans are very charismatic with outgoing personalities. They have many friends but don't feel connected to them. Although they are forward thinking, they are rigid and may judge others harshly and come across as very cold and unfeeling. People may wonder if Atlanteans are even human!

Even though they are aware they are different and brighter than others, they still tend to conform and gravitate towards mainstream professions such as science, programming, and philosophy. They tend to be workaholics, placing much importance on status, wealth, luxury, and manifesting. They are excellent problem solvers and, therefore, very adaptable but want to be the boss and delegate tasks. Although they can be very technology-oriented, they also make great energy workers and mediums. They attune to and can teach about crystals and are great channelers, especially of intergalactic information.

Physically, Atlanteans are tall and attractive with mesmerizing, hypnotic eyes. Because of their charisma and appearance, they can be very persuasive. They tend to fear water and natural disasters and are prone to headaches, especially when forced to do mundane tasks. They are very vulnerable to dark energy and do their best to avoid it as they perhaps sense the high probability an entity may attach to them.

Atlanteans may always feel they don't fit in and feel a nagging desire to *go home*. They tend to gain weight as a way of grounding themselves to the here and now. To bring them into balance, they would benefit from working on their heart chakra to offset their detachment from others and their overactive third eye and crown chakras.

Arcturian Starseed

From the star Arcturus in the Bootes Constellation, the handle of the big dipper points to the bright star of Arcturus. It is a red orange supergiant star located 36.7 light-years from Earth in the Bootes constellation. Arturians lived many lifetimes in Atlantis where early crossbreeding began. They look a lot like us and have similar DNA.

Arcturians bring us ancient wisdom from Arcturus, which is our galaxy's most advanced civilization. They often do this through the use of sacred geometry. They are the leaders and doers instead of the empaths or feelers. They tend to be more practical than other starseeds. They are fantastic at public speaking. They also deal with a strong shadow side.

Orion Starseed

Orions originate from the Orion Constellation and Orion Nebula. The belt of Orion was revered in Ancient Egypt as the symbol of Osiris and the three main pyramids of Giza align with these three stars, creating a gateway to Heaven. Orions are quite diverse in their appearance and may have reptilian traits. However, they typically are given the stereotype of having a big head and big eyes.

Orions are the truth seekers. They are easily identifiable by their incessant questions about everything. They are often misjudged as aloof because they hide their emotions due to a lack of trust. This lack of trust stems from being dominated by the darker beings known as the Greys, who value greed and power. They love and help us with technology, science, and medicine while they learn to trust again.

Orions have a very healthy dose of self-confidence. Due to this self-esteem issue, some have flipped and helped the Reptilians. They are the masculine representation of the polarity where the Sirians and Pleiadians would be the feminine; just as the Atlanteans would be the masculine and the Lemurians would be the feminine. This masculine energy brings (in the traditional sense) the emotionless and logical side. They have a reputation for ruthlessness with a mission to teach government, business, industry, politics, and military systems. They are highly competitive, driven, magnetic, logical, confident, and successful.

Before you make the mistake of thinking they are not spiritual, they play an important role in protecting the Akashic records and providing balance. Their Orion Light Council is one of the highest galactic councils, along with the Andromedan Council.

THE FLIP SIDE

While a few flip side extraterrestrials are listed below, let me make clear my position on them. My position is that there are people who can contrive all kinds of stories, and while they may believe it as truth, what I know is this—Reptilians and Draconians do not give a flying flip what we think about them (unless that energy grows into a thought form). But basically, they do not care. Do I have flip side stories? Yes, but that is better saved for another time and space.

Draconian Starseed

Draconians comes from the Draco constellation, which is only 303 light-years from Earth. Draconian starseeds are associated with dragons and are a subrace of the Reptilians. As with any beings, there are some benevolent Draconians who wish to help Earth evolve and there are malevolent Draconians whose only intent is to use our resources for their own gain and personal power. The evil Draconians seem to far outweigh those that have evolved for good. Draconians are very military-like in energy, and they intend to multiply and conquer.

Reptilian Starseed

Reptilians (Lizard People, Saurians, and Draconians) originate in the Draco Constellation, Earth, and Orion. They descend from Draconians and have reptilian features. However, they are master shape-shifters.

These spirit beings are perfect examples of duality. They helped humans evolve and survive while on the other hand they seek to control Earth. It is said they seek to control us through political means and that many are here on Earth living as humans. It is almost as if they possess humans in the way demons do. There are many types of Reptilians but the Draconians (geneticists of sorts that seek to perpetuate their DNA) and Earth Reptilians (wisdom keepers, but who manipulate emotions for their agenda) are the most common.

Practice
Which Starseed Are You?

The following true or false exercise will help you narrow down which starseed(s) you are or which type you work with as guides or spirit beings. For every true statement in a section, give yourself one point. Remember that there is a strong chance you are a hybrid of more than one.

Like any of these simple quizzes, try to answer honestly as opposed to what you want to be. In fact, it is always good to let someone who knows you well also take the test on your behalf. Also remember that there are many more starseeds and that we are all starseeds playing our part. No one is more important than the other (but perhaps that is my Pleiadian and Lemurian coming out and wanting everything to be even).

Whichever starseeds have the most totals are most likely your true form (the type of starseed you are) or the ones who work with you. The answers to the quiz are found in the appendix.

Group A

1. I am drawn to multidimensional beings such as unicorns or Sasquatch.
2. I feel like I can communicate telepathically.
3. I am naturally connected to aquatic life.
4. I am drawn to Egypt and Egyptian history.
5. I have deep interests in science.

6. I consider myself an artist and creative person.

7. I like to analyze and watch people.

8. I have a few close friends recognizing quality over quantity.

9. I love fantasy and science fiction.

10. I consider myself a mystic, witch, or healer.

Total:

Group B

1. I am psychic.

2. I am an empath.

3. I often have lucid, powerful, vivid dreams that often are premonitions.

4. I am led by my heart.

5. I have a more feminine nature.

6. I struggle with low blood pressure and low body temperature.

7. I am concerned with humanitarianism.

8. I do not see the point of social hierarchy.

9. I have a sensitive immune system and can easily develop auto-immune disorders.

10. I am an extremely loving individual and can easily love to a fault.

Total:

Group C

1. I value freedom above everything else.

2. I love change, and like moving all the time.

3. I have an intense sense of adventure.

4. I can astral travel and connect to higher dimensions.

5. I have a calling to help people expand and awaken their consciousness.

6. I love a simple life.

7. I am humble and low key—confident but not showy.

8. I am often described as an old soul.

   9. I am a private person.

10. I am called to be a teacher and guide of this world.

Total:

Group D

1. I am science-minded with a high interest in physics, biology, and molecular science.
2. I am a futurist. I believe in the integration of biology and technology.
3. I easily tap into the higher spiritual realms.
4. I channel messages from the higher realms.
5. I am often in contact with high vibrational beings.
6. I feel a sense of connection to the collective consciousness.
7. I support sustainable resources and businesses.
8. I promote and encourage health practices that could lead to the raising of a person's vibration.
9. I am drawn to help others heal in mind, body, and spirit.
10. I am aware that a multidimensional consciousness and ascension is possible even while on this earthly plane.

Total:

Group E

1. I am very analytical.
2. I work towards goals and see them through with passion.
3. I fight against injustice with a passion.
4. I am fiercely independent.
5. I am athletic.
6. I am a fearless daredevil.
7. I am very grounded. My root chakra is strong.
8. I enjoy life to the fullest.
9. I tend to be assertive, direct, and self-sufficient.
10. I possess keen survival skills.

Total:

Group F

1. I have a muscular physique, and I am physically strong and powerful.
2. I am logical, intellectual, and analytical.
3. I like to compete and have a competitive nature.
4. I speak my mind and I am not afraid to express my opinions.
5. I am confident.
6. I have a strong thirst for knowledge.
7. I seek evidence and quantitative proof before buying into a belief.
8. I often favor logic over emotions.
9. I am a perfectionist.
10. I need alone time to recharge.

Total:

Group G

1. I am sensitive to light.
2. I prefer warm weather.
3. I am cold all the time with no real medical reason.
4. I tend to have a dominant, assertive personality.
5. I am a night owl.
6. I am persuasive, observant, and methodical.
7. I am charismatic and/or witty.
8. I have a distinct order to my values.
9. I have an RH- blood type.
10. I do not like to be disrespected.

Total:

Group H

1. I have a strong interest in technology.
2. I am curious how crystals power watches and computers.
3. I have premonitions of natural disasters.
4. I like order and calm.

5. I know there is negativity in the world because I have experienced it.
6. I am claircognizant—I know things but don't always know why.
7. I channel spontaneously.
8. Some people consider me cold or aloof.
9. My physical body feels heavy and dense.
10. My healing comes more through energy work than through body work.

Total:

Group I

1. I love crystals.
2. I can communicate telepathically or feel I used to do so.
3. I love dolphins and whales.
4. I believe in a society where everyone is on equal footing.
5. Hearing about arguments and wars hurts my soul.
6. I feel free about romantic relationships.
7. I feel many spirits around me.
8. I have an addictive personality.
9. I know plants are beings and I communicate with them.
10. I don't always feel that I am the same person I was when I was born.

Total:

Group J

1. I know good and evil exist on Earth.
2. Sometimes I feel torn between what is right and wrong.
3. I find I do not really like Earth or many humans that much.
4. I am drawn to military things.
5. I like dragons.
6. I believe we have free will in how we behave.
7. Sometimes I want to have more power than I feel I have been given.

8. I believe some species are meant to guide and even rule over others.

9. Sometimes I feel anger come over me that is hard to control.

10. I believe political hierarchy is important for social order.

Total:

CONNECTING

The best way to connect to multidimensionals is to learn about their habits and peculiarities. Once you have become familiar it is easier to adjust your frequency to theirs. It makes no difference if they are in human or spirit form because you will connect with them based on their frequency.

Practice
11 Steps for Automatic Writing
to Connect with Your Galactic Guides

The following is a form of channeling to help you connect with your galactic guides through automatic writing.

1. Get into a state of relaxation (usually through meditation) that is almost like a trance but still allows you to participate by asking questions and writing.

2. Have a journal dedicated to automatic writing, with a pen or pencil close by, to contact your galactic guides.

3. Have a specific question for a guide. You do not need to know which guide, but if you want to choose one to connect with that is fine.

4. Begin to write down everything that comes into your mind. Do not leave anything out. Don't worry about punctuation. Just let the writing flow! (Some people will suggest using your non-dominant hand to write in order to get your logic out of the way. If this appeals to you then try it. For some it may prove too frustrating.)

5. You can ask your galactic guides anything but remember they are on a much higher frequency than you typically operate. They are concerned with the advancement of civilization, but they still might be interested in what color car you want.

6. Adjust your frequency to the type of multidimensional you are working with in your automatic writing.

7. Do not dismiss anything as too outlandish and do not judge it. You might receive messages from the flip side unless you strongly set your intention not to receive those messages.

8. You might want to record the information you receive because it comes so quickly you cannot write it all down. While some will claim this defeats the purpose of automatic writing, who cares? Rules do not really apply when dealing with these high vibrational beings.

9. As you advance, try to not put limitations on your guides. See what messages come through and remember you have free will to listen to the guides or not to listen.

10. Be prepared for a wild ride.

11. Don't freak out, or the session will shut down because of a change in your frequency.

PROTECTING

The primary thing to remember with most multidimensionals is that they are right here among us. You probably have the DNA of one or several of them. If you decide to work with their energy, you now know from the attributes described in this chapter what you are dealing with at least most of the time.

However, these spirit beings are extremely advanced and have learned what we have not—everything is energy and can transmute into any form. Therefore, do not always go by how someone looks to you. That is a mistake we often make in life. Base your dealings with these beings on their vibration. Don't worry too much about connecting or protecting; it's more likely you will pop out of their energy the minute you become afraid anyway because you are no longer matching their frequency.

Collaborating

We already collaborate with multidimensionals whether we realize it or not. Our energy is inextricably entangled with the energy of all that is.

HONORING

The best way to honor a multidimensional is to treat them as you would any other guest that is here to help us evolve. If they are here to cause us harm, then clearly do not honor them.

Practice
11 Ways Multidimensionals Can Help You

The following will show you ways that multidimensionals can help you. You can consider these and journal about how the various multidimensionals may interact in your life now.

1. Lyrans help you have both a strong work ethic and a strong pursuit of adventure.
2. Andromedans help you realize you can consciously ascend while on Earth.
3. Sirians help you enjoy animals on Earth as well as the multidimensionals such as unicorns or Sasquatch.
4. Pleiadians help you realize that your purpose is not what you do for a living. Your purpose is what you contribute to the evolution of Earth's consciousness ascension.
5. Lemurians help you realize you are just as important as anyone else.
6. Atlanteans help you learn to utilize technology for advancement.
7. Arcturians help you get things done while overcoming shadow side fears such as public speaking.
8. Orions help you realize that it is okay to be successful. Failure does not make you more spiritual. The key to success or failure is how you deal with it.
9. Draconians help you keep thirst for power in check.
10. Reptilians remind you of the duality of all spiritual beings.
11. All multidimensionals will help you put life into perspective. Call on the energy of any of these beings just as you would an archangel or any other type of guide.

DEMYSTIFYING

I propose that all of us are starseeds. Our higher selves did not originate here on Earth and most of us have incarnated many more times than the Earth is old. So, not only are we all *star stuff* as Carl Sagan says[12], we are all starseeds. Some of us long for our original home while some of us are comfortable on Earth. So, you see, we are all extraterrestrials of some sort.

Perhaps the days of laughing at those who believe in aliens are over. The Pentagon has admitted to UFO sightings, and while this does not mean they have admitted to extraterrestrials, many of us really do not need the government to know that they already walk among us.

. . . .

12. Carl Sagan, *The Cosmic Connection: An Extraterrestrial Perspective,* Produced by Jerome Agel (Garden City, NY: Anchor Press/Doubleday, 1973), pp. 189-190.

11
Astral Travel, Parallel Universes, and Doppelgangers

When I was growing up, I lived in a town about two hours from Dallas, Texas. We would travel to a Dallas suburb almost every summer to go to an amusement park known as Six Flags Over Texas. While I have never enjoyed rollercoasters or heights, I still looked forward to this annual trip.

It can get very hot in Texas and one year I had a heat stroke. I recall feeling very dizzy and faint as I stood by the ticket area where visitors enter the park. I did not feel like myself at all. I had to find a place to sit down and try to feel better. As I sat there, I watched people going in and out of the public restrooms, which were located nearby.

Fast forward one year—we came to the park and were going through that same ticket area, when an overwhelming sense of déjà vu came over me. Obviously, I had been in this spot just the year before, but this was something completely different. I began looking around and as I looked toward the restrooms, I discovered they were not restrooms at all—they looked like old saloon doors instead. As I continued to watch, I saw something very surprising. A version of myself dressed in western clothes holding a woman's hand was entering the doors into the saloon. Mesmerized, I began to walk toward the saloon doors intending to follow "myself" inside when I heard someone call out my name telling me to quit wandering away from the group.

Every single time I go to that Six Flags, I see that saloon and that version of myself, but I am never able to actually go inside.

FLIP SIDE

Many times, we talk of shadow sides or that part of ourselves we hide from everyone else, including ourselves. If we take into account that only part of our entire soul self is in one place and other parts may be in other places, parallel universes, or even lifetimes, then some aspect of ourselves might be living out the duality that inhabits all energy.

When I was in my self-destructive phase in life, I was working on criminal defense cases. One night, I was trying to fall asleep but there were beings that had circled around my bed. These were not kind beings. They were in dark cloaks and had no faces. They were as real as you are as you sit reading this book. They continued to just stand around the bed staring at me. Finally, I telepathically told them that I really needed to sleep and promised them I would travel in my dreams with them if I could just get physical rest. I fell asleep almost immediately.

I astral traveled with this group of beings. As promised, I met them in the dream space. But I was a different aspect of myself. I was a hooded killer with no face. I swept over towns and killed those who did not follow the hooded ones. I killed without remorse or hesitation.

Although this was and is part of me now and was happening while I slept, it was also in the future. The future exists now in some parallel realities.

I still see the stares of the hooded ones. In fact, I myself have a stare of pure energy that when misdirected can cause great harm. I am very aware of this aspect of my energy; it is one reason I work to manage it. You see, there is duality and polarity in all of us, and in a parallel universe we may find that we are not the person we are in this aspect of our beingness.

INTRODUCING

I propose that only part of your entire energetic soul being is currently in this particular plane of existence. Other parts of your higher self, or your energetic self, are in other parallel bodies in multiple dimensions and parallel realities. When part of your entire energetic soul being decides to incarnate on Earth, we think of it in terms of reincarnation of a single soul who has also had other past lives. In truth it is just one aspect of you who has chosen from millions of possible alternative experiential choices. You have an infinite number of selves experiencing an infinite number of incarnations that may include past, present, and future lives. Because time is not linear, they all can be happening at the very same time.

There are spirit beings that live and walk among us that are also from the past, present, and future. Thanks to physics we are now beginning to learn about how time folds in on itself and how it is possible to exist in parallel universes simultaneously. A parallel universe, also known as an alternate universe or reality, is a self-contained plane of existence, co-existing with one's own current universe or reality. Parallel universes are another copy of our universe.

All potential parallel universes combined constitute what is known as a multiverse. In other words, our universe is not the only universe. There are other universes—some of which may play out alternate versions of this one. Sometimes these universes blend into one another, and what seems to be an ordinary person may actually be a time traveler.

Humans are not alone in their ability to astral travel. A good friend, Carla, told me recently about an experience she had witnessing the astral projection of a friend's little Papillon, Woodrow. Woodrow belonged to her life-long friend, Freda, who lived in another state. Woodrow was infatuated with one of Carla's three dogs, Kelani. When the friends were together along with their dogs, Woodrow was constantly at Kelani's side and simply would not or could not leave her alone. He did not do this with either of Carla's other two dogs, only Kelani.

Due to a multitude of circumstances, the two friends had been unable to visit one another for a couple of years when Kelani developed a severe back issue, basically paralyzing her hips and back legs and taking away her ability to walk. It was quite serious, and it initially appeared that she would not recover without back surgery, which Carla did not want to impose on her. Carla had talked to Freda about what was going on quite frequently, trying to decide what she should do.

One day, while in her kitchen, Carla saw what she assumed was one of her other two dogs in her peripheral vision. However, it caught her attention because something about it seemed off. She then looked down and realized that both of her dogs were at her feet. (Kelani was in a pet stroller.) She shrugged it off, assuming it was her cat, Felicity, who is in spirit and that Carla often sees and/or feels with her. She knew it hadn't looked like Felicity but that was the only explanation she could think of at the time.

This happened several more times and she caught enough glimpses to finally recognize who it was she was seeing. Woodrow! This concerned her because she was afraid something was wrong with him and that was why she was seeing him repeatedly. She decided to call Freda to check on him only to find out he seemed perfectly fine. It then dawned on them that he may have picked up on the fact that something was wrong with Kelani and perhaps it was possible he had been able to astral project to check on her! Freda found the thought quite amusing and so asked him, *Woodrow, do you ever go and visit Kelani and check on her?* The little white Papillon went absolutely NUTS at the question! Whether he understood what she was asking or simply thought she was asking him if he wanted to go visit her is irrelevant. The point is that even after a couple of years and hundreds of miles distance between them, he knew and loved Kelani and wanted to be with her.

Did he astral project and do just that? I believe he did 100%. I know how easy it is to astral project and see absolutely no reason why animals can't do it as well. His emphatic reaction to the question is proof enough for me!

IDENTIFYING

Because our universe is so incredibly large with trillions of galaxies spinning through space, each made up of trillions of stars, the concept of multiverses—those outside, parallel, or mirroring ours—while not hard to believe, can be very hard to wrap our brains around. Thankfully, scientists specializing in quantum mechanics have begun to wrap their scientific brains around these concepts and are proving that multiple states of existence are not only possible but more than probable due to something they call wave function, which supports all these theories.

The principles of wave function say you could be living completely different versions of your life simultaneously, and because you can only see one version at a time you would not have the slightest clue. You could also be living the same day over and over again and be clueless to the fact you are trapped in your own version of *Groundhog Day*.

Just as there is more for scientists to discover about the wave theory, there is much more for each of us to consider regarding our own perception of our 3D universe and reality. With an open mind and an open *third eye*, we may discover for ourselves how much more there is to discover within our own personal *reality*. By learning how to astral project and travel, we are opening up a myriad of possibilities for exploring the present reality, a parallel reality, or even the past, the future, or a completely different universe. The possibilities are endless as are the opportunities to learn more about what is truly *real*.

Astral travel and astral projection are terms that are often inappropriately used interchangeably to describe out-of-body experiences. To avoid confusion, we will use the term *astral projection* to describe the process of your spirit leaving your physical body and *astral travel* to refer to leaving the current physical location to travel somewhere else. Those destinations can be within this 3D plane or to a parallel plane or universe.

When you astral project, your spirit pulls out of your body and can go anywhere you want it to go, but your physical body does not go anywhere. It is my belief that the more you learn to astral project, the more you will find yourself able to connect with various types of spirits. Keep in mind that due to the multidimensional nature of astral travel, you may meet *doppelgangers* along the way. Doppelganger means *double walker* and is a double of a living person. It may appear as an apparition, or when astral traveling as a living version of someone you recognize from another reality, even yourself!

Astral travel/projection can happen intentionally or unintentionally while awake or while asleep (lucid dreams). A practice will be provided at the end of this chapter that will give you step-by-step instructions for a process to intentionally astral travel when awake. To intentionally astral travel during sleep, all you have to do is set the intention to have lucid dreams before you go to sleep.

Lucid dreaming is the experience of being fully aware during a dream that you are asleep and dreaming. You probably have experienced this but may not have realized it was different from other dreams in that you are not merely an observer during a lucid dream, you can learn to navigate within the dream, go where you want to go, interact with whom you want to interact with and, more importantly, are not at the mercy of the dream if you don't like the direction it is headed. You have the power to simply change it or go no further and simply choose to wake up.

With practice, lucid dreaming is easily accomplished and for beginners who want to astral travel it is a good place to start. Just be consistent in setting the intention each night before you go to sleep and don't get discouraged if it doesn't happen on your first attempts. Eventually, you will be successful, I can assure you!

Astral projection sometimes happens spontaneously without setting the intention to do so. This usually occurs during the dream state when you have a lucid dream, but it can also happen when you are in a meditative state or when you are experiencing a disruption to your normal state of perception such as illness or trauma.

Basically, astral travel/projection is a process where there is a disconnection of the spirit from the physical body. The astral body is then free to move around at will, no longer encumbered by a physical vehicle, and you are able to journey to a multitude of destinations, including other worlds. This is referred to as an out-of-body experience.

Practice
11 Steps to Astral Travel

The following walks you through steps to astral travel.

1. Find a time and place where you will not be interrupted. Silence all mobile devices and preferably turn them off completely and/or have them in another room. (Interruptions can be quite jarring.)

2. Get physically comfortable. Adjust or change your clothing, take off your shoes and jewelry and try to remove any potential physical distractions.

3. Find a comfortable chair that allows you to sit upright, spine straight, or if you prefer you can lie down. This brings up a point regarding astral travel: Many people believe you need to tether to earth so you won't get lost when you astral travel. I know from experience with certainty that there is no need to tether. If that is true, make sure you do it before using anesthesia because you certainly travel when put under.

4. Begin by focusing on your breath while slowly inhaling deeply through your nose and then exhaling slowly through your mouth. When you feel fully relaxed, move onto the next step.

5. Set an intention of where you would like to go in your astral travel. Use your imagination to try to envision this destination

in your mind's eye. Try to envision as many details as you possibly can and engage as many senses as you can—sight, sound, smell, and touch. Remain aware of any emotions you feel (i.e., peace, happiness, curiosity or even fear or sadness).

6. Explore this place to your heart's content, taking note of everything you experience. If you see any other people or beings, try to discern if they can see you or are aware of your presence.

7. If you encounter anyone who seems to be aware of you, try to gauge their reaction to your presence (i.e., whether they realize you are an astral traveler or simply think you are someone from within their "reality," whether your presence frightens them or makes them uneasy, etc.).

8. Remain respectful of this place and considerate to anyone you encounter. If appropriate, you can communicate with anyone you meet, but choose your words carefully so as not to alarm them should they not realize you are a *traveler*. Remember, when connecting to spirits of a different vibration, their way of communication may also be different.

9. More often than not, you will be only an *observer* within this other plane of existence and may not be able to do more than observe, so be sure to pay close attention to as much as you can in order to benefit as much as possible from this experience.

10. When you are ready to return home, simply set that intention. You will immediately find yourself back in your body. Do not make any sudden movements or open your eyes as it can be too harsh of a *re-entry*.

11. Sit quietly for a few minutes. Slowly bring your awareness back to your physical body. Begin to wiggle your fingers and toes, stretch your muscles, and return fully to the present moment, time, and place. When you are ready, open your eyes.

NOTE: If you want to connect with yourself in a parallel universe, it is important to incorporate very specific intentions before beginning your astral journey. Just as you would when traveling using your car's navigation system, you need to be very specific in setting the parameters around your astral trip as well.

PROTECTING

Many people have perpetuated fears about astral travel and astral projection. As someone who has done both for as long as I can remember, I can assure you these fears are the stuff of Hollywood. First, let me make one thing very clear: While we are all one and corded to everything and everyone, we do not have some silver cord that connects us to our physical body like an astronaut does when floating around in space. Our mind is what connects us. We can visualize these cords of connection, but do not be afraid that it is going to be severed and you will be forever lost in the astral plane. It makes for a good horror story, but it is bunk.

Second, people try to claim that you are vulnerable to possession if you astral travel. You have no more likelihood of becoming possessed by a spirit while astral traveling or projecting than you do at any other time. Frankly, I would be more concerned about going under anesthesia for surgery. You are much more vulnerable to psychic attack when in a drug-induced state than when your mind is fully functioning.

Third, people also fear-monger regarding all the different types of beings you might encounter while in the astral realm. Hopefully by now you have gotten the message from this book that there are all kinds of spirits moving among us all the time! They are not limited to or confined to the astral realm.

Fourth, people worry about dying while they astral travel. Rest assured, there is no ill effect on your physical body caused by astral projection. In fact, astral projection can be very beneficial to anyone who is ill or experiencing trauma by disconnecting the mind from the physical or emotional pain the physical body is experiencing. That being said, your physical body is still vulnerable to death even when your spirit is elsewhere. So, to that extent, it is possible you could die while your spirit is astral traveling, but it would not have been the cause.

Finally, one caveat: There is something you may need to protect yourself from in regard to astral travel. It is possible to develop a tendency to want to check out of your body all the time. This is not healthy for you. After travel, be sure to ground by connecting with nature and staying present. If you have a job to do in the astral realms, then do it. But there is a reason you are on Earth, so honor that commitment and try to remain present the majority of the time.

COLLABORATING

If you do encounter someone you believe to be from a parallel universe, or a time traveler, do not think you are crazy. You are not. You may see yourself coming and going. You may catch glimpses of other frequencies. While no one, not even the brightest minds in the world understand it all, I do believe you can make every effort to communicate with these beings and try to discover how you can help them, how they can help you, or you can both help humanity.

HONORING

I will absolutely roll out the red carpet for any spirit being that has come into my consciousness. It is more a matter of trying to learn from them and appreciating what they have accomplished.

DEMYSTIFYING

Always keep in mind these spirits are real even if not in true physical form. One thing to consider is that they may be confused. Approach them cautiously to give them time to adjust to the frequencies. Find a way to communicate even if it is telepathically. Remember, most of us communicated telepathically at one point, so some part of our being still knows how. Keep in mind that we don't have a complete understanding of how time bends in on itself as so much of this remains unproven. However, there are many scientific theories that appear to support all of what I have proposed here.

What I do know with certainty is that Earth, the Universe, and the multiverse are full of spirits because I have seen them for myself. I am here to tell you that you can see and interact with them too. There is no veil. There are only the self-imposed limits we put on our perception, limiting our ability to see and to soar. If you can remove those limits, you will begin to perceive the spirits among us and have the ability to connect and interact with them, and once and for all, dispose of the veil.

Conclusion

I am a history buff and enjoy hotels with character. The Brown Palace Hotel and Spa in Denver, Colorado, is one such hotel. While finishing my second draft of this book, Roger and I stayed there to visit the local gem and mineral show. The hotel has a rich history of visiting presidents, posturing socialites, scandalizing murders, and entertaining ghosts. I have seen plenty of spirits at this hotel, but none of the ones advertised or rumored to live there.

Ghosts love to mess with elevators. You know how kids will press all the buttons—spirits do that too. A hotel historian, an intoxicated guest, and a resident ghost in waiter attire were all in the elevator with us one night. The elevator was stopping on every floor, and the door would open to no one. Finally, the inebriated guest exclaimed *it must be the ghosts!* The historian and Roger started talking about the hotel's history, and the intoxicated guest became wide-eyed and got off at the next floor. I just looked at the full-bodied waiter ghost and smiled as he pushed more buttons.

I immediately thought, what a perfect summary of how people deal with spirits. Some will joke about them but run scared when confronted with their reality. Others will discuss the fascinating history and would probably know what is all around if they just adjusted to the spirit's frequency. Yet others immediately see the spirit and feel a kindred nature with them.

Throughout this book, I have attempted to impress upon you that this world is crowded. There are spirits of every kind all around you. The only issue is how you want to interact with them, because they interact with you. Perhaps you have come to realize you play host to many spirits and that you may even create some of your own. Always remember that your imagination is a spirit's playground, and you hold the key. No veil or rules need to confine how you communicate with spirits, because you are the portal to everyone and everything you can ever dream.

Resources

Please visit me at www.michellewelch.com for many more ways to explore the spirits around you and to find activities relating to the promotion of this book.

Appendices

The appendices contain additional information expanding upon things that were discussed in the body of this book. These are the topics you will find here:

- Planes, Dimensions, and Realms
- Chakras
- Auric Fields
- Clairs
- Crystals for Archangels
- Feathers
- Starseed Quiz Answers
- Who You Gonna Call?

Planes, Dimensions, and Realms

You may have heard people refer to the *different planes of existence*. While we cannot with any authority know that this theory is entirely accurate, it does seem to explain some of the different types of interactions we as physical beings may experience with spirits in the nonphysical realms. There seems to be some disagreement regarding the actual number of planes of existence. Still, for our purposes, we can simplify things by considering five: physical, etheric, astral, mental, and causal.

The physical plane is just as it sounds. It is the densest frequency of existence and includes space, time, energy, and matter. The physical plane is linked to the next plane, the etheric plane, which is comprised of *life force* energy. The two planes co-exist, so when the physical body dies, the etheric body within the etheric plane also ceases to exist. (Or, you could also say that the life force energy of an individual moves on to the next plane of existence—the astral plane—when the physical body dies.)

The next plane of existence is the astral plane. The astral plane is where the spirit goes when it leaves its physical body. This plane can also be accessed from the physical plane through astral projection, meditation, near-death experience, lucid dreaming, or spirit communication.

The mental plane is a plane where consciousness exists unencumbered by physical matter. Thought is no longer generated by the mind, which relies on words and language. In the mental plane, communication becomes instantaneous through a form of energy exchange based on frequency. Manifestation of thought is immediate, so higher vibrational forms of angels, ascended masters, and guides reside here. This may explain the phenomena of instantaneous channeling some people experience when accessing it from the physical plane.

Finally, the causal plane is the highest plane and the foundation of all existence. It is the highest of vibrational frequencies and comprised of what is often characterized as Divine Source.

Within these different planes, there are a wide variety of spirits that vibrate at many frequencies. And while we often want to label these spirits as good or bad, in truth, the difference between them simply comes down to a difference in vibrational frequency. On top of that, an individual spirit's primary frequency may fluctuate from time to time. For example, what we would typically characterize as a lower vibrational being may at times choose to vibrate at a higher frequency. Other spirits may, in some situations, decide to lower their vibration.

As we begin to discuss how we as physical beings can interact with nonphysical forms of energy, we must consider why we would want to do so. As human beings living in this physical plane, our experiences are closely related to our frequency. The physical plane is where the densest energy frequencies reside and why it is a plane of form and matter.

Suffering and struggle result from the lowest frequencies within this plane, and that part of us that experiences it is known as ego. We will never feel complete and whole as long as we are in the ego's grip. However, if we can manage to transcend the ego and instead operate from our higher selves, we will begin to feel in a state of oneness and perfect contentment due to achieving a much higher (and less dense) frequency. Our ultimate goal then, if we want to avoid as much suffering as possible, is to attempt to operate from our higher selves rather than merely struggling to survive and overcome in this physical world.

Detecting, connecting to, and collaborating with nonphysical spirits while living in the physical is potentially an excellent resource for us. Not only is receiving guidance on how to navigate our lives beneficial but collaborating with high vibrational spirits can help to elevate our vibrational frequency. As intimidating as it may sound to you, it is not that difficult to connect to nonphysical spirits. It is simply a matter of aligning yourself with the vibration of the energies you choose to mingle with or entertain.

Please realize that when you successfully begin to elevate your frequency there are some potential pitfalls. Ego is not easily defeated and is always ready to undermine you. One of these pitfalls is thinking that "you have arrived" and are fully awakened. This is ego, pure and simple. With very few exceptions (e.g., Jesus, Buddha, Dalai Lama, etc.), you no longer reside in the physical plane of existence once thoroughly awakened. So, if you are still here, it is because you still have the cares of the world to deal with, and ego has, in fact, not been transcended.

Finally, it is worth mentioning that while all these ideas I am presenting are simply theories that cannot be proven, they strongly resonate as accurate for me. That being said, they may or may not resonate as accurate for you. Just keep in mind that neither logic nor science has explained everything about how energy, life force, and spirit work. Likewise, faith and belief have not been able to explain all aspects of them either. However, science and faith are coming closer as quantum physics begins to validate concepts that were once only theories. Perhaps now we are beginning to open our minds to the oneness of all that exists and the entanglement of energy.

In the metaphysical sense, planes are levels of existence. First, there are the main three: etheric (physical), causal, and astral plane. The etheric (also known as the physical) is thought of as that closest to Earth. It is the densest plane and is where humankind currently resides. As mentioned previously, space, time, energy, and matter are recognized. Here we are deluded into thinking we are separate from one another and everything. Fear dominates this plane and could have the lowest vibration.

The second plane of existence is the astral plane. It is made up of emotional energy. It is said to be where our consciousness resides after death and where we spend some time before moving onto a higher sphere. It is believed to be the realm of disembodied souls and those that are non-human such as lower angels, guides, and elementals. This is where the spirit goes when it leaves its body. There are no bodies or physical forms in the astral plane, only spirits. It is believed to be the realm of disembodied souls, but other types of spirits also dwell here.

Lower angels, various types of spirit guides, elementals, extraterrestrials, and many other energy beings exist in the astral plane. Each level in the astral plane is separated by different vibrational frequencies. Consider this: What people label good or bad, Heaven or Hell, is just so-called planes with varying frequencies in their vibration with higher or lower frequencies. Everything in existence exists as vibration.

Ultimately, we can choose to vibrate and exist at any level. In that sense, all energy beings, including us, can shape-shift. Logic and science have not explained everything. Faith and belief have not explained everything. But perhaps they are coming closer and closer together in quantum physics and metaphysics now that we are at least opening our minds to the oneness of all and the entanglement of that energy.

What is most important is to know that our ultimate goal is to align ourselves with the vibrations of the energies we choose to mingle with or entertain. When we realize that our ultimate goal, purpose, or will is to operate from our higher selves versus that part of us merely trying to survive and overcome this world (known as ego), we will feel complete and whole. We will feel in a state of oneness and perfect contentment because this is what our higher selves and a higher frequency will bring.

Please note that even when we feel or experience this awakening, we haven't arrived. We still have the cares of the world to deal with, and there are times we will need to operate in duality and ego when on this Earth. We are given ego for a reason, just as there are lower vibrations for a reason. Not all the reasons are to be judged and summarily dismissed.

A dimension is technically a pair of opposite directions—length, width, height, and time. By traveling along with that space, you end up in another space or dimension. You did not travel to it. You traveled through it to reach an alleged inaccessible space. A dimension is not another universe. It is another direction or time. A realm is a kingdom. It is where you live or reside. The most accurate word is brane, short for membrane, a term from quantum physics that represents spaces apart.

The fact that everyone uses the words plane, dimension, and realm interchangeably does not matter as long as you understand that everything is energy and it oscillates or vibrates. In other words, no matter what dimension, plane, or realm energy is moving in, it is moving at a specific rate called frequency. Learning to adjust your frequency is how you will interact with all the varying spirit beings around you.

Chakras

The word *chakra* comes from Sanskrit, the secret language of India. It means *wheel* or *turning*. Chakras are centers of awareness in the human body found in the subtle energy system. They are means by which various energy fields exchange energy. This energy is what connects us to all the many surrounding and varying frequencies of energy vibrations.

The chakras have been described as funnel-shaped and extend out in front of and behind your body. In India, chakras came to be pictured as lotus blossoms. However, different people see chakras differently, including cone-shaped spirals, horns of plenty, and spinning 3D spirals. The chakras each have individual functions, but it is essential to know that they all work together. The chakras promote harmony between one's inner and outer worlds by connecting and aligning with varying frequencies.

In traditional writings, there are up to 88,000 chakras; however, most people deal with the seven principal chakras aligned on the spinal column. Seven is a sacred number to many people. The secondary chakras in the hands and feet are often considered important. They are called *nadis*. Nadis are actually in all chakras and throughout the body, but most people just focus on the ones in the hands and feet. In the hands, they are primarily in the middle of your palms and are directly connected to the heart chakra. The foot chakras lie in the middle of the soles of the feet and are directly related to the root chakra.

As we introduce the seven primary chakras, it helps if you think of the colors of the rainbow. Think of the colors of the rainbow—ROYG-BIV. Colors and chakras go together, and once you learn to think in terms of color and chakra, many other things become very natural to intuitively understand, such as archangel, candle, and crystal associations.

First Chakra—Root (Base)—You Are Secure
Color—Red

Location—Base of the spine or the area of the tailbone

Purpose—Survival, security, stability, and self-preservation

Element—Earth

Sense—Smell

Body Parts—Bones, skeletal structure

Glandular Connection—Adrenals

Emotional Dysfunction—Mental lethargy, spaciness, restlessness, difficulty achieving goals, basic fear, lack of trust

Physical Dysfunction—Constipation, back pain, bone disease

Animal—Elephant

Foods—Proteins, meats, root vegetables

Fragrances—Cedarwood, cloves, musk, patchouli, rosemary, vanilla

Crystals—Agate, bloodstone, garnet, hematite, onyx, red jasper, ruby, smoky quartz, tiger's eye

Herbs—Elderberry, lime blossom, valerian

Flowers/Trees—Clematis, rock rose, sweet chestnut

Instrument—Drums

Second Chakra—Sacral—You Are Vital

Color—Orange

Location—Two finger widths below the navel

Purpose—Creativity, fertility, passion, sensuality, sexuality

Element—Water

Sense—Taste

Body Parts—Bladder, circulatory system, prostate, sex organs, womb

Glandular Connection—Ovaries and testes

Emotional Dysfunction—Unbalanced sex drive, instability, addiction, feelings of isolation

Physical Dysfunction—Impotence, bladder/prostate issues, lower back pain, kidney disease

Animal—Fish

Foods—Liquids

Fragrances—Jasmine, rose, rosemary, sandalwood

Crystals—Amber, aventurine, carnelian, citrine, fire opal, golden topaz, moonstone

Herbs—Nettle, parsley, yarrow

Flowers/Trees—Oak, olive, pine

Instrument—Percussions

Third Chakra—Solar Plexus—You Are Worthy

Color—Yellow

Location—Below base of the sternum (just under ribs)

Purpose—Willpower, self-confidence, self-esteem, self-control, your power center

Element—Fire

Sense—Sight

Body Parts—Digestive system and muscles

Glandular Connection—Pancreas and adrenals

Emotional Dysfunction—Need to be in control, over sensitivity, addictive personality, aggression, low self-esteem, insecurity, sleep disorders

Physical Dysfunction—Stomach ulcers/ailments, fatigue, weight around the stomach, allergies, diabetes, digestive problems

Animal—Ram

Foods—Complex carbohydrates

Fragrances—Bergamot, carnation, cinnamon, rose, vetiver, ylang-ylang

Crystals—Amber, apatite, citrine, sunstone, tiger's eye, topaz, yellow jasper

Herbs—Chamomile, fennel, juniper

Flowers/Trees—Hornbeam, impatiens, scleranthus

Instrument—Stringed instruments

Fourth Chakra—Heart Chakra—You Are Loved

Color—Green (traditional) and pink (modern)

Location—Center of chest

Purpose—Love, compassion, empathy, humanity, tolerance, openness

Element—Air

Sense—Touch

Body Parts—Chest, circulation, heart, lungs

Glandular Connection—Thymus

Emotional Dysfunction—Co-dependency, melancholy, fears concerning loneliness, commitment issues, poor boundaries, problems with relationships

Physical Dysfunction—High or low blood pressure, coronary and respiratory disease, shallow breathing, cancer

Animal—Gazelle/antelope

Foods—Vegetables

Fragrances—Bergamot, honeysuckle, jasmine, rose, tarragon

Crystals—Aventurine, azurite, chrysoprase, emerald, green calcite, jade, malachite, rose quartz, watermelon tourmaline, ruby zoisite

Herbs—Melissa, thyme, whitehorn

Flowers/Trees—Chicory, red chestnut, roses, willow

Instrument—Bowed instruments

The Fifth Chakra—The Throat Chakra— You Are Heard

Color—Blue

Location—Central throat

Purpose—Communication, verbal ability, expression, universal truth

Element—Ether/Akasha

Sense—Hearing

Body Parts—Ears, mouth, neck, nose, teeth, throat

Glandular Connection—Thyroid and parathyroid

Emotional Dysfunction—Perfectionism, inability to express feelings, shyness, not being heard

Physical Dysfunction—Thyroid ailments, neck pain, speech defects, sore throat, hearing or ear issues, tinnitus, asthma

Animal—Elephant/bull

Foods—Fruit

Fragrances—Camphor, chamomile, eucalyptus, lavender, myrrh, peppermint

Crystals—Aquamarine, blue lace agate, blue topaz, celestite, lapis lazuli, sapphire, sodalite, turquoise

Herbs—Coltsfoot, peppermint, sage

Flowers/Trees—Agrimony, cerato, mimulus

Instrument—Voice

The Sixth Chakra—The Third Eye or Brow Chakra— You Discern Truth

Color—Indigo

Location—Above and between the eyes

Purpose—Awareness, imagination, insight, intuition, realization, wisdom

Element—Light and telepathic energy

Sense—Sixth

Body Parts—Eyes, the base of the skull

Glandular Connection—Pituitary

Emotional Dysfunction—Nightmares, learning difficulties, hallucinations, anxiety, poor concentration

Physical Dysfunction—Headaches, poor vision, neurological disturbances, dizziness

Animal—Spirit totem

Foods—None

Fragrances—Cajeput, hyacinth, lemongrass, rose geranium, violet, white musk

Crystals—Amethyst, apophyllite, azurite, lapis lazuli, lepidolite, moldavite, opal, sapphire

Herbs—Eyebright, spruce, St. John's wort

Flowers/Trees—Crab apple, vine, walnut

Instrument—Woodwinds

The Seventh Chakra—The Crown— You Are Connected to All that Is

Color—Violet

Location—Top of the head

Purpose—Spirituality, the experience of higher planes, enlightenment, self-realization, cosmic consciousness

Element —Cosmic energy

Sense—Beyond self, cosmic awareness

Body Parts—Upper skull, cerebral cortex, skin

Glandular Connection—Pineal

Emotional Dysfunction—Depression, obsessive thinking, confusion, flight from reality

Physical Dysfunction—Cancer, immune system disorders, chronic illness

Animal—Multidimensional or hybrid spirit

Foods—Fasting (none)

Fragrances—Frankincense, lavender, rosewood

Crystals—Amethyst, clear quartz, Herkimer diamond, lepidolite, selenite

Herbs—None

Flowers—Wild chestnut, wild rose

Instrument—Gong

Auric Fields

Your aura is the energy field that surrounds your entire body. Everything has its aura, and often we can sense a person's auric field when we pick up on their vibe. Your aura is connected to the seven energy centers of the body called the chakras, and is comprised of seven different layers. Each of these layers will vary in depth and size, depending on the person and where they are at in their lives. In a healthy state, the entire aura can extend several feet and is very bright in color. In an unhealthy or weakened state, the auric field can be small and dull. The aura layers pulsate outwards from the body, with the first layer being closest to the body and the seventh layer being farthest away from the body.

Each layer also increases in vibration as it moves outwards, with the seventh layer carrying the highest vibration. A nonphysical being is the aura or life force. We may see the pure aura and swirling energy, or we may perceive the energy in a physical form.

1st Layer: Etheric

- Closest to the physical body
- Represents the physical body, muscles, tissues, bones, etc.
- Connected to the root chakra
- A bluish grey color
- Easiest to see with the naked eye
- Pulsates at 20 cycles per minute
- Stronger in athletes and those who are very active
- Weaker in those who lead a sedentary lifestyle or when immunity is compromised

2nd Layer: Emotional

- Second from the physical body
- Represents emotions and feelings
- Connected to the solar plexus chakra
- Can be all the colors of the rainbow

- Can be muddy colored during times of emotional stress
- State of the chakras can be easily determined from this layer

3rd Layer: Mental

- Third from the physical body
- Represents thoughts, cognitive processes, and state of mind
- Bright yellow in color
- Connected to the sacral chakra
- Often radiates the strongest around the head, neck, and shoulders
- Stronger in those who engage in mental tasks or those who have an overactive mind
- When engaging in a creative activity, colored sparks can also be seen flowing from this layer

4th Layer: Astral

- Fourth from the physical body
- Represents where we form our astral cords with others
- Pink or rosy in color
- Connected to the heart chakra
- Becomes stronger through loving, intimate relationships
- Can be weaker during breakups or conflicts with loved ones
- State of the chakras are also easily visible from this layer

5th Layer: Etheric Template

- Fifth from the physical body
- Represents the entire blueprint of the body that exists on this physical plane
- Includes everything you create on this physical level including your identity, personality, and overall energy
- Connected to the throat chakra
- Can vary in color
- Healed and made stronger by expressing your truth and knowing who you truly are

6th Layer: Celestial

- Sixth from the physical body
- Connected to the third eye chakra
- Carries a very strong and powerful vibration
- Represents the connection to the Divine and all other beings
- Where unconditional love and feelings of oneness flow
- Pearly white in color
- When strong, the person may have the ability to communicate with the spirit world and receive angelic messages
- Can be healed with unconditional love

7th Layer: Ketheric Template

- Farthest away from the physical body (estimated around 2-3 ft. away)
- Represents the feeling of being one with the universe
- Holds all the information about your soul and previous lifetimes
- Vibrates at the highest frequency
- Connected to the crown chakra
- Gold in color
- Rapidly pulsates
- When strong, gives you the ability to surrender to the path of the Divine and can help increase psychic abilities

Clairs

The following explores in more detail various forms of psychic ability.

Clairvoyance—Clear Seeing

Clair means *clear* in French, and voyance means *vision*. Clairvoyance is the ability to gain information through means of seeing pictures. The pictures may be seen visually (like we see right now) or through visions/pictures in the mind's eye. The latter way is far more common. The mind's eye is visual memory or imagination and is also known as the third-eye or sixth chakra. When seeing with the mind's eye, it may feel like a memory, but you are actually seeing the future. Some call this remembering the future. Clairvoyance without the mind's eye is typically seen in mediums who are primarily born with this gift of seeing spirits in tangible form. If you have this gift, you already know it.

Clairsentience (Empath)—Clear Feeling

Clair means *clear* in French, and sentience means *feeling*. Thus, clairsentience is a form of extrasensory perception where one acquires knowledge primarily through empathic feelings and emotions or by feeling what is going on with another person emotionally. This empathy mirrors someone else's emotions and can often confuse the one sensing it until they learn to manage their energy. This is discussed thoroughly in my book, *The Magic of Connection*.

Clairaudience—Clear Hearing

Clair means *clear* in French, and audience means *hearing*. Clairaudience is the ability to hear in a paranormal way. It doesn't always refer to actual sound but may be sound in the *inner mental ear,* much like how people think words without having auditory impressions.

Clairaudience is primarily used to receive guidance from spirits. You can be clairaudient in two ways: audibly or with your inner ear. A sound from your inner ear feels like it is coming from your inner being. It is not information you are reaching for or trying to remember. It is information you receive. It feels like when you hear a song you know in your inner ear or a conversation from the past.

Clairaudience with the *outer ear* is hearing spirit audibly. This can sometimes be quite startling. You will know a difference in the voice. Spirit usually uses this only in times of urgency, such as a voice yelling that there is a fire but later no one can find the person who gave the alarm.

Claircognizance—Clear Knowing

Clair means *clear* in French, and cognizance means *knowing*. Claircognizance is a form of extrasensory perception where knowledge is acquired without explaining how one understands the information. It is the ability to know things without pictures or hearing and with very few details as to why. It is one of the least talked about clairs but is probably the most common.

Five Signs of Claircognizance:

1. You have always just known things—even as a child
2. You have always known if things are good or bad ideas but can't explain why
3. You just know if you should do things but can't explain how you know
4. The knowing is strong, but the details are vague
5. You just know!

Clairtangency—Clear Touching (also known as Psychometry)

Clair means *clear* in French, and tangency means to *touch*. Clairtangency is the ability to handle an object or touch an area and gain psychic knowledge through energy about the article, the owner, or its history. This ability is much more common than people realize. Many people think of small objects, but it can apply to large things such as buildings.

Clairgustance—Clear Tasting

Clair means *clear* in French, and gustance means to *taste*. Therefore, clairgustance allows you to taste a substance without putting it in your mouth, thereby obtaining psychic knowledge through taste. This is probably one of the least utilized psychic senses, but it is useful for spirit communication.

Clairscent—Clear Smelling (also known as Clairolfactory)

Clair means *clear* in French, and scent means *smell*. Clairscent is where a person acquires psychic knowledge primarily by smell. This is also one of the least utilized psychic senses but is very useful for spirit communication.

Crystals for Archangels

Archangel Ariel (animals, the environment, and physical needs)

- Rose quartz represents her pink aura. Rose quartz is a stone of unconditional love.
- Green moss agate is also ideal for connecting with her energy. It is an excellent stone when working with nature or the environment.
- Red jasper and hematite are excellent stones for the root chakra. Because Ariel helps us with our physical needs, crystals directly related to our root chakra are beneficial.

Archangel Azrael (comfort for those grieving or dying)

- Yellow calcite represents his pale yellow or off-white aura. Yellow calcite is a very uplifting stone, making it the ideal stone for Azrael because it uplifts those grieving. It enhances meditation and induces a state of relaxation.
- Apache tear, which is a form of black obsidian but is much gentler, is another stone that comforts during times of grief.

Archangel Chamuel (helps find what you seek)

- Green fluorite is an excellent crystal to connect with Chamuel and his pale green aura. Fluorite has a stabilizing effect, it teaches the importance of balance and grounding, helps with the focus that is needed to find things when they are lost, grounds excess energy and helps with emotional trauma, absorbs negative energies in the environment, and brings information up from the subconscious mind and accesses intuition. It brings order to chaotic situations, which is precisely what Archangel Chamuel will help you do when seeking something.

Archangel Gabriel (helps with children/fertility/adoption, communication, and creativity)

- Copper represents Gabriel's dark orange or copper aura. If you are drawn to it, you can be sure Gabriel is working with you. Copper is also a "feel better" element. It brings vitality and luck. It also helps with emotional balance.
- Carnelian helps with vitality, creativity, and fertility.
- Turquoise, blue lace agate, or any sky-blue stone are excellent to help you speak your truth. These crystals that help get a message across will also draw in Gabriel.

Archangel Haniel (helps with poise, grace, clairvoyance, and moon energy)

- Moonstone connects with Haniel's light blue aura and moon energy. Moonstone is also strongly connected to intuition and clairvoyance. It soothes the emotions and helps with virtually all feminine issues.

Archangel Jeremiel (helps with emotional healing)

- Amethyst is perfect for connecting with Jeremiel. Jeremiel not only has a sparkly, purple aura, (s)he is the Angel of Prophetic Visions and Dreams. This makes amethyst the perfect stone for Jeremiel because amethyst is one of the most spiritual stones, and it helps with sleep and dreams. It is also suitable for overall protection.
- Celestite is ideal for meditation, dreams, and visions associated with Jeremiel.

Archangel Jophiel (helps those in any creative field, helps bring beauty and joy)

- Rubellite is a red form of tourmaline. It is the color of fresh raspberries. Pink rubellite is a beautiful bright pink. Pink rubellite is a stone of balance and calm. It brings emotional balance and helps you open up, relax, and detach from personal pain. It directly touches the heart.

- Bright fuchsia agates are also great to use when working with Jophiel.

Archangel Metatron (helps children and helps clear chakras with his cube)

- Watermelon tourmaline links the heart chakra to the higher self. It is a *feel-good* stone that is great for love, fun, and humor. This makes it an excellent stone for children; therefore, perfect for Metatron.
- Ruby zoisite is also an excellent stone to use with Metatron.
- Sugilite is also associated with Metatron because it helps children with learning difficulties.

Archangel Michael (the great protector, helps lightworkers)

- Sugilite is an excellent stone to represent the royal purple and because it is a stone of courage that Archangel Michael instills in us. It is also a *love stone* that brings the purple ray to Earth. It inspires spiritual awareness and wisdom.
- Lapis lazuli and dark amethyst are also good to connect with Archangel Michael. Both Lapis lazuli and amethyst are crystals of great protection and royalty.

Archangel Raguel (helps bring harmony to relationships)

- Aquamarine is a very soothing stone that connects with Raguel's soothing pale blue aura. It harmonizes its surroundings just as Raguel brings harmony and mediates disputes. Also, it helps invoke tolerance of others. It is also a crystal of courage to help those who protect the underdog, just as Archangel Raguel does.

Archangel Raphael (helps with all healing and traveling)

- Malachite connects with Raphael's green aura and is a crystal that heals and helps with pain. It is one of the best healing crystals. It builds your physical health by strengthening your heart. It also brings calm and emotional balance. Because of Raphael, malachite is known as a crystal to carry with you when you travel.

Archangel Raziel (helps with psychic abilities, past lives, and esoteric material)

- Clear quartz is ideal to represent the iridescence of Raziel. It is a crystal that improves quality of life and can be programmed for any situation. It channels any energy, thereby helping any condition. It is an amplifier of all other stones and also brings clarity to any problem. Some quartz crystals are record keepers, and there are many different geometric shapes, so it is the perfect crystal for Raziel.
- Labradorite is a magical stone that stabilizes the aura and the chakras. It has beautiful rainbow coloring that calls in the magic of Raziel.

Archangel Sandalphon (grounds between physical and spirit, soothes with music)

- Turquoise represents the color of Sandalphon's aura. Additionally, it blends the energy of material and spirit.
- A Shaman's stone, it heals the spirit and brings about wisdom, trust, and kindness. This stone is also a healing and protection crystal.

Archangel Uriel (illuminates truth)

- Amber is ideal for Uriel not only due to the aura color, but also because it is good for the memory and intellect. It is also great for manifestation. Strictly speaking, amber is not a crystal at all. It is a tree resin that solidified and became fossilized. Amber also brings spiritual wisdom as does Archangel Uriel.

Archangel Zadkiel (helps with compassion and forgiveness)

- Lapis lazuli is a crystal that represents the dark blue aura of Zadkiel and brings vitality and wisdom. It is one of the best stones to work with the brow chakra (third eye), and it is sometimes used to balance the throat chakra. Lapis lazuli is a crystal of protection. It brings the enduring qualities of honesty, compassion, and uprightness to the personality. It is suitable for relationships and can help with forgiveness.

Feathers

As mentioned in chapter 3, it has been described for so long that angels have wings and feathers that this is what people expect, so angels may leave feathers for us as a sign. Likewise, spirit guides and loved ones may also utilize feathers as a way to send us a sign. Here are the meanings behind the colors of feathers.

>**White Feathers**—White feathers are a beautiful sign of peace and serenity. They let you know that your guides are with you and watching over you. If you see a white feather, let it bring you comfort.

>**Red Feathers**—Red feathers represent love. Your guides are letting you know that you are loved or that love is on its way to you.

>**Pink Feathers**—Pink feathers represent unconditional love and friendship. Your guides are letting you know that you are loved. A light pink feather could also be a message from Archangel Ariel, and a dark pink feather could also be a message from Archangel Jophiel.

>**Orange Feathers**—Orange feathers represent creativity and passion. This passion includes your sex life. Orange is a color of vitality. Your guides are reminding you that it is never too late to pursue whatever sets your soul on fire. This could also be a message from Archangel Gabriel.

>**Yellow Feathers**—Yellow feathers are *feel-good* feathers. Your guides are sending you an uplifting message of joy and reminding you to enjoy life. You are worthy of every good thing. Take a moment of mental clarity and enjoy all the happiness in the present moment. This could also be a message from Archangel Uriel.

>**Green Feathers**—Green is the color of health and nature. Your guides are telling you to get out in nature to connect with the elementals and take care of yourself. Nurture and nature are the things to remember with green feathers. Green feathers can also indicate abundance coming to you. This could also be a message from Archangel Raphael.

Blue Feathers—Blue is the color of the water that brings about serenity. Your guides are sending you a message to do what needs to be done to bring about peace in your life. This may mean clearing the air with someone by telling them how you feel. It could also mean that you have talked enough, and now it is time to listen and accept the outcome. Blue feathers also represent your psychic awareness. Sky blue can also be associated with Archangel Raguel, turquoise may also be a message from Sandalphon, dark blue may be a message from Zadkiel, and dark blue with purple may be a message from Michael.

Violet Feathers—Violet or purple feathers are about spiritual growth. Your guides are telling you to get in touch with your higher purpose in life. Or perhaps they are acknowledging how far you have come on your spiritual journey. These feathers may also indicate a message from Archangel Michael.

Brown Feathers—Brown is the color of dirt, soil, and the earth. Your guides are reminding you to be yourself and not lose sight of your earthly purpose. In other words, get your head out of the clouds now and then see the blessings all around you on Earth.

Grey Feathers—Grey feathers represent balance or neutrality between two opposing forces. Things are in the grey area. There is no clear answer. Nevertheless, it is an indication of balance and impartiality.

Black Feathers—Black feathers often appear as a warning or show you that your guides protect you and have your back. Do not assume they mean bad luck. Set your intention that if you see a black feather, it is a sign from your guides to be careful, use wisdom, and call upon them for protection.

Black and White Feathers—Black and white feathers indicate duality and choices. You may need to make a decision soon. The feather is a sign that while there can be balance, a choice may need to be made for your peace of mind.

Spotted Feathers—A spotted feather indicates that it is time for a change. Stop procrastinating and make up your mind. It is time to let go of the past.

Starseed Quiz Answers (chapter 10)

Following are the answers to the chapter 10 quiz, "Which Starseed Are You?" The starseeds with the most totals are most likely your true form (the type of starseed you are) or the ones who work with you. Refer back to chapter 10 for more information once you know your answer.

Group A—Sirian
Group B—Pleiadians
Group C—Andromedans
Group D—Arcturians
Group E—Lyrans
Group F—Orions
Group G—Reptilians
Group H—Draconians
Group I—Lemurians
Group J—Atlanteans

Who You Gonna Call?

Many times, the scariest beings in our lives are the humans living in our homes or somehow involved in our lives. Here are some resources.

Suicide
1-800-SUICIDE or 1-800-784-2433
1-800-273-TALK or 1-800-273-8255
TTY 1-800-799-4889
Text HOME to 741-741 for free 24-hour support from the Crisis Text Line
Outside of the U.S., please visit the International Association for Suicide Prevention for a database of resources.

Domestic Violence
1-800-799-SAFE (7233)
TTY 1-800-787-3224
Text "START" to 88788

National Sexual Assault Hotline
1-800-656-4673 (HOPE)

Trans Life
1-877-565-8860

Bibliography

"Collective Unconscious." Definition and Facts. britannica.com. britannica.com/science/collective-unconscious, accessed November 20, 2021.

Deegan, Gordon. "Fairy Bush Survives the Motorway Planners." *The Irish Times.* May 29, 1999. www.irishtimes.com/news/fairy-bush -survives-the-motorway-planners-1.190053, accessed November 20, 2021.

Horowitz, Dr. Leonard and Joseph Puleo. *Healing Codes for the Biological Apocalypse.* Tetrahedron Media, LLC. June 16, 2021. 58-61, 345-6.

Jung, C.G. *Two Essays on Analytical Psychology*, Collected Works of C.G. Jung, Volume 7. "The Structure of the Unconscious." Princeton: Princeton University Press. 1972. 263—292.

Jung, C.G. *Synchronicity: An Acausal Connecting Principle*, From Volume 8. of the Collected Works of C. G. Jung. Princeton: Princeton University Press. November 14, 2010.

Jung, C.G. *Structure and Dynamics of the Psyche*, Collected Works of C.G. Jung, Volume 8. "The Significance of Constitution and Heredity in Psychology." Princeton: Princeton University Press. 1970. 229—230.

"Law of Relativity." Law of Relativity - Laws of the Universe. weebly. com. https://lawsoftheuniverse.weebly.com/law-of-relativity.html, accessed November 20, 2021.

Sagan, Carl. *The Cosmic Connection: An Extraterrestrial Perspective.* Produced by Jerome Agel. Garden City, NY: Anchor Press/Doubleday. 1973. 189-190.

"The Spiritual Law of Duality." thesoulmedic.com. https://www .thesoulmedic.com/the-spiritual-law-of-duality/, accessed November 20, 2021

Welch, Michelle. *The Magic of Connection.* Woodbury, MN: Llewellyn Publications. 2020.

Wundt, Wilhelm. *Element der Volkerpscholologie: Entwicklungsgeschichte Der Menschheit.* Whitefish, MT: Kessinger Publishing, LLC. 2010. 116.

Index

U

unbalanced, 180
unconscious mind, 9, 79, 80, 93
undine, 92, 93, 95, 97
unicorn, 84–87, 146, 151, 158

V

veil, 2, 3, 6, 7, 14, 64, 72, 114, 115, 131,
    144, 169, 171
vibrate, 4, 15, 22, 23, 81, 134, 175–178, 187
vibration, 6–8, 10, 11, 14, 22–28, 31, 35,
    39, 43, 47, 48, 54, 55, 64, 72, 81, 88, 92,
    94–96, 101, 106, 111, 112, 114–116,
    118, 119, 122, 127, 128, 134–136, 142,
    143, 146, 153, 157, 167, 176–179, 185,
    187
Virgin Mary, 46
Vishnu, 35
Vision, 21, 47, 65, 88, 98, 99, 101, 163,
    183, 189, 194
visiting spirits, 109
vitality, 88, 194, 197, 199
vulture, 84, 86, 87

W

Walt Disney, 36, 38, 40
wasp, 84, 86, 87
water elementals, 96, 97
waterfall scrying, 98
wave scrying, 98
whale, 84–86, 88, 155
windchimes, 67
wisdom, 3, 9, 49, 56, 58, 88, 133, 145, 149,
    151, 183, 195–197, 200
wolf, 79, 84–87
woodpecker, 84–86, 88
worm scrying, 98

Y

Yoruba Orisha, 33

Z

zebra, 84–87

TO WRITE TO THE AUTHOR

If you wish to contact the author or would like more information about this book, please write to the author in care of Llewellyn Worldwide Ltd. and we will forward your request. Both the author and the publisher appreciate hearing from you and learning of your enjoyment of this book and how it has helped you. Llewellyn Worldwide Ltd. cannot guarantee that every letter written to the author can be answered, but all will be forwarded. Please write to:

Michelle Welch
℅ Llewellyn Worldwide
2143 Wooddale Drive
Woodbury, MN 55125-2989
Please enclose a self-addressed stamped envelope for reply,
or $1.00 to cover costs. If outside the U.S.A., enclose
an international postal reply coupon.

Many of Llewellyn's authors have websites with additional information and resources. For more information, please visit our website at http://www.llewellyn.com.